Shift Your Standards

Shift Your Standards

The how-to-guide for navigating life after University: Learn how to create your dream reality and thrive in your 20s.

Michelle Lynn Johnson

10th House Publishers

Shift Your Standards
The how-to-guide for navigating life after University: Learn how to create your dream reality and thrive in your 20s.

Michelle Lynn Johnson
Copyright © Michelle Lynn Johnson 2024
Published by 10th House Publishers

Paperback ISBN: 979-8-9912338-1-1

Disclaimer

This book is designed to provide competent, reliable, and educational information regarding health, mental and physical, and wellness. However, it is sold with the understanding that the author and publisher specifically disclaim all responsibility for any liability, loss, or risk, personal or otherwise, incurred as a consequence, directly or indirectly, of the use and application of any of the contents of this publication.

Taking the steps to work on oneself is a courageous one. This publication contains content that may be potentially triggering or disturbing. Individuals who are sensitive to certain themes are advised to exercise caution while reading. The use of any information provided in this book is solely at your choosing and risk.

Know that the author has shared her tools, practices, and knowledge with you with a sincere and generous intent to assist you on your journey. Please contact her at Info.michelleljohnson@gmail.com with any questions you may have about the information she provided. Michelle will be happy to assist you further and be an ongoing resource for your success.

Table of Contents

Part 1:

Life Lessons and Advice

Michelle Lynn Johnson

You just graduated college, now what?

Welcome to the guide to tackling post-graduation life that has nothing to do with what you might currently think postgrad life entails. In this book, I will not teach you how to create the best resume, nail an interview, or create a top-notch budget. I will not be barking at you with lists of "to-do's" postgrad or how to ensure you negotiate the best 401k plan. While those concepts may have been the focal point of most of the postgrad advice you have heard thus far, I am here to show you an entirely new way of thinking about your future.

In this book, I plan to share advice that will change how you see the world forever and change the person you will become.

A common theme among many people dealing with a postgrad crisis involves the idea that life will never be as good as it was during college. Older adults are feeding you the lines, "Enjoy it, life only gets worse from here," or, "Good luck getting a job in today's market, no one is hiring right now."

Not only do students hold all of these different fears about what will happen after graduation, but college grads have to leave the community they've been a part of for four years. When you are used to living with friends, walking across the hall to socialize whenever you feel like it, and having endless fun activities at your fingertips, it can be quite isolating when you finally have to let go of that lifestyle.

For many, they will move back in with their parents. They may have few or no friends left in their hometown. This can be an extremely challenging transition for graduates, and it's not talked about enough.

Although this isn't everyone's experience, it is very common for graduates to deal with extreme stress, anxiety, and even depression after graduating. Postgrad depression is real for so many people, even those who may have never dealt with mental health struggles in the past.

This can look different for everyone, there is no one-size-fits-all. It could be watching months of your life go by after graduation and not accomplishing anything.

It could be spending summer days in bed staring at job search websites. It could be avoiding socializing because you don't have the energy, or you don't feel like explaining why you haven't gotten your dream job yet.

It could also be landing your dream job but still wondering why you don't feel happy. Maybe you seemingly have it all together on paper: moving to a new city you always dreamed of, having your dream job in place, and finally having money in your bank account. Still, though, it might feel like something is missing.

Whatever your experience is, I am here to validate you. This is *normal* to experience during this transition, even if you don't feel like it is. If you have felt stuck for months or even years after graduation and are carrying that shame with you for not yet thriving postgrad, this book is for you. Or maybe you are about to graduate, and you're terrified of it, this book is also for you.

The experience I want to prevent you from having is to make decisions just for the sake of lessening the pressure, and not because you want to do it. The longer you stay in a situation you hate, the more you will lose inspiration for your dreams. The days go by, and eventually, that excitement you had for your future diminishes. It becomes hard to see how things can be different or better.

You don't have to go through this alone. I have crafted this book specifically for you because I know what it's like to feel everything you are feeling. After years of learning my life lessons as well as researching endlessly, I truly believe I have found the steps and information that can change your life postgrad.

This book is a different approach to getting on your feet than you may have been expecting, but I promise you it's for a good reason. We aren't focusing solely on career-oriented advice in this book because, truthfully, your career is not going to be what gets you through life's difficulties. You cannot thrive in life if your mental health is on the back burner. I'm here to teach you how to create a life that excites you, NOT just how to look good on paper to those around you.

I'm going to share with you my personal experiences and story, as well as everything I have found to be true about postgrad life. I hope this will help you feel less alone and more validated in your experience. Sometimes, it can be healing in itself to know that someone else sees you and understands what you are going through. I hope you will see me as a good friend who has your back, not just someone telling you what to do. I am happy for you to take the advice that resonates and leave what doesn't yet resonate. This path is yours and the right things for you will stand out.

I am here to be your tour guide through navigating all of the newness you are experiencing. A tour guide is someone who provides insight and information so the person they are guiding gets the most out of their experience. I want to make your journey of exploring postgrad life one you can sail through with maybe just a few waves along the way instead of taking the uncertain route that may include six-foot waves and capsize your boat. My wish is to make your exploration through your 20s one where you don't feel entirely lost and alone, where if you need to grab a hand to get you through a hard time, you have mine to grab onto.

In the second half of the book, I will share with you the steps you can take to start changing your life now. These will be real, actionable things you can do today to get on your way to the life you have always desired. Having a sense you are making progress in your life will help you get out of feeling stuck and lost, even if it's small progress. You will learn how to build a relationship with yourself that will sustain you through the rest of your life. You will learn how to create a mindset that will allow you to be strong through life's hardships. You will learn how to create long-lasting habits without giving up. You will learn how to discover the parts of your current mindset that are holding you back.

Michelle Lynn Johnson

The goal of this book

When people compare themselves to others, there is this idea that the other person is seemingly "perfect," and you are below them in some way.

There are many people you probably look up to; your therapist, an author who has multiple best-selling novels about getting your life together, that influencer you followed who made incredible changes in their life, a celebrity, or that well-dressed person you saw walking the street during their lunch break.

Since you look up to them, it can be easy to think they don't have bad days and have figured some secret out about life that you have yet to discover.

I want you to listen closely. There is no secret recipe to becoming a perfect individual who has it all together. There is, however, a recipe for building resiliency.

The majority of people on this Earth don't speak about what they are going through. Most people do not want to burden others with their problems. Or they don't feel safe speaking to others about their dark thoughts and feelings. Out of sight, out of mind. If we do not see for ourselves someone expressing the difficulties of their lives, we naturally assume they don't have any.

But the fact of the matter is everyone struggles and has bad days. Everyone has searched the internet and bought books in hopes of finding the answer to life that someone else has figured out. Everyone has laid in bed a little longer in the morning because they felt too sad to get up. Everyone has wondered why they are sad when there seemingly isn't a reason. It is part of being human.

As I have been writing this book, I have had my bad days. And oftentimes when I have one, I think, "Well who am I to write this book about changing your life when I am still having bad days." Thoughts are weird like that because when they come up, you want to think they're true because they're from your brain.

7

I always remind myself of this; your thoughts *do not* hold any truth unless you *decide* they do. You are not your thoughts. Your brain feeds you all different thoughts for a variety of reasons, **none** of those reasons being that you are an unworthy or incapable person.

The **real truth** I make sure to shift my thoughts to during those negative spirals is thoughts like, "I might have bad days, but I do know how to prioritize myself. I know how to nurture myself and get through it instead of lingering in it like I used to. My bad days aren't the end of the world for me anymore, I accept them when they come, and I have a deep faith in my heart that they will pass." Because THAT is my truth, *not* the negative thoughts that my mind sometimes still wants to feed me. I get to decide what is my truth, and not every thought that pops into my mind reflects that.

When people pick up self-help books, I think it's pretty common for them to think, "Ok, this book is it. This book will hold the solution to life not being hard anymore." And when it's not, they buy ten more self-help books after that, hoping one of them will fix them in the way they want to be.

What you might not understand yet is that you aren't broken or lost, you only *feel* that way right now. But the truth is you aren't, deep down inside you are whole just as you are. You were always whole; life just got in the way and made you feel otherwise. I want this book to teach you about your inherent wholeness and how to return to your **true** self.

Changing your life can be pretty simple—it can come from a few perspective shifts and action steps forward. I want you to understand that you are already enough the way you are, you might not have reached far enough within yourself to pull that belief out yet. I will teach you how to do that.

You will learn how to embrace your humanness and be resilient in the face of it. With our humanness come our bad days, like the ones I still have and the ones everyone you look up to still has. With our humanness comes heavy emotions and hard thoughts. But we always have a choice when we feel bad: we can dwell in our sadness and sit in it, or we can flow through it and out of it.

I am here to teach you HOW to get through the difficulties you are facing in your 20s, not how to make the difficulties stop forever. The difficulties *will* come. But they will also *go*, and they will go a lot quicker when you know how to flow through them and be adaptable in the face of them.

What truly matters after graduation

When you begin your transition into life after college, you will inevitably feel a lot of different emotions at once.

Everyone believes if you can land the perfect job postgrad then all of your problems will be solved. There is a surplus of financial advice online such as: how to start paying off your student debt, creating a budget, and negotiating your salary. However, it doesn't address what college graduates are really dealing with.

The truth is, landing the perfect job **will not fix** the heavy emotions you are feeling due to transitioning into "real" adult life. The job cannot fix the loneliness, grief, anxiety, or stress you may be experiencing.

You can quite literally be the most successful person right out of college making tons of money, but if you had to walk away from the community at a school you loved, you are still experiencing a loss.

Your mental health should be at the top of the list of priorities. I promise you will be okay if you decide to take a little bit of time to just be. To simply decompress and process this new change. You will not ruin your career if you take a break. You will not fail, you will not be a disappointment, you will not be behind.

I want to make it clear that I am **not** diminishing the importance of setting yourself up for financial success or creating a sustainable career, I am simply putting focus on another extremely important conversation that shouldn't be placed last in terms of priority level, like it usually is. There are plenty of books and people who created the conversation around all of that other stuff, it's just not part of what I am emphasizing here.

I want to share this research with you to help put into perspective how important prioritizing your relationship with yourself, others, and your mental health is. Based on the National Institutes of Health, here are the top five regrets of the elderly before they pass away:

9

"I wish I'd had the courage to live a life true to myself, not the life others expected of me."
"I wish I hadn't worked so hard."
"I wish I'd had the courage to express my feelings."
"I wish I had stayed in touch with my friends."
"I wish I had let myself be happier."

I want you to think about these. You can see how within those regrets, no one was worried about their career or finances. What your job is and the money you had in the bank isn't going with you to the grave. No one will talk about how rich or how poor you were at your funeral. No one will talk about how many Instagram or TikTok followers you had. People are going to talk about the person you were, how you made them feel, the hobbies that made you, you, and the impact your character left on this world.

No one regrets the six months/one year they took off in their 20s to figure it all out, mess it up, learn about themselves, start over, etc. What matters most is your ability to be courageous, your ability to take care of yourself in the way you deserve, your ability to be vulnerable with those you love, the connections you have that should be cherished, and your willingness to allow yourself to feel good.

I truly believe that if you master the art of a relationship with yourself, your career, the finances, and all of those things will come with much more ease. When you are resilient and persistent, when you ooze self-love and love for others, and when you are courageous and passionate you will be the type of person who has the dream career.

Better yet, the stronger you are within yourself and the more you get to know yourself, the more likely you are to know exactly what you are meant to do here in this world. You will know what your natural gifts and strengths are.

Panicking about what is to come in life, shoving away all of the heavy emotions that come from graduating college and never allowing yourself to truly feel them, and operating from a place of shame daily due to the fact you can't stop feeling behind, *will only keep you where you are*. If you land your dream job *it will not change* the fact that you're dealing with some very heavy emotions. It will not change your relationship with yourself. Your salary won't change your character or your relationship with those you love.

There's a lot to think about as a young adult. One of those things is considering what is truly important to you in this life. What do you value the most? Is it family? Is it being able to help others? Is it feeling free and alive? Is it love?

You don't have to think about it all at once, though. One thing to understand about becoming an adult on your own is that there aren't any rules to living. If you don't want to do something, no one can make you. This is both a blessing and a curse. The blessing is that you get to be the one who creates your life, but the curse is that if you don't decide to act, no one is there to do it for you.

Now that you understand the purpose of this book, join me as I share my story of how I found my path after college graduation.

Michelle Lynn Johnson

My Journey

As an author writing a book about helping you thrive postgrad, I want you to get to know me as a person so you, the reader, can understand why I am writing this for you, and why I am so passionate about helping you.

I want you to know a little bit about my heart, my experiences in life post-graduation, and the journey of how I became the person I am today. The person who was once in your shoes.

I'll just go ahead and dive right in, because is there any other way to jump into the part of the book where you share your greatest struggles with strangers all over the world for the first time?

Well, here goes nothing!

I was incredibly privileged to have the college experience I did, it truly was a dream come true. Just like the one you see in the movies that makes you so excited to graduate high school and start college. I was a Division I athlete on the equestrian team at Sacred Heart University in Fairfield, CT, which was an amazing aspect of college for me. I met all of my best friends on this team, everyone was family no matter if you were a freshman or a senior. The number of laughs and bonding moments we shared in the car going to practice 40 minutes away from campus multiple times a week or waiting by the cubbies in the gym before strength and conditioning were endless. I got to travel with the team to competitions around the country as we made it to the semifinals every year, which were always out of state. I made memories on those trips I will never forget. One such memory was when our coach had us wear matching bright red Adidas tracksuits in the airport—we got asked if we were the gymnastics team, basketball team, cheerleading squad, or anything but what we were. I remember giggling with my friends about the silly questions strangers would ask us. Or the time we were all out to eat in North Carolina in a diner and my friends snapped what we thought back then, was the most hilarious picture of me of all time, and we were sobbing laughing at the table while our coaches looked at us thinking we were crazy.

I was a marketing major in the business school and had most of my classes with two of my best friends, so going to class was fun for me as well. There wasn't much about college I didn't like, besides that it had to end. Of course, there were *plenty* of moments of stress from schoolwork deadlines, and the pressure of being a Division I athlete, but the good times made it so I never focused on any of that. Honestly, when I look back on my experience, I don't think of the schoolwork because the life experience, friendship, and personal growth were what had the most impact on my life. Although I had many late nights writing papers, failed tests that felt like the end of the world at the moment, and hard courses I had to study endless hours for, I was never really in it alone. I'd spend those hours in study hall at a table with all of my friends who were in the same boat. We'd stress cry together and then go out for McDonald's McFlurrys after. The feeling of community was like nothing else I'd ever had.

Fast forward to the end of my four years in May 2019. I had to come to terms with the fact that my identity could no longer be summed up in a small phrase such as, "Hi everyone, I'm Michelle and I'm a marketing major and on the equestrian team at Sacred Heart." As it turned out, the actual day I walked the stage for my college graduation ended up being one of the most significant days of my life, but not in the way you might think. It went like this…

I woke up to the sound of rain ferociously hitting the old, peeling windows of my bedroom in my college house. Disoriented, I shot out of bed and grabbed my phone with a pit in my stomach, terrified that I was going to be late. Good thing the sounds of the rain had woken me up from the deep slumber I was in because I forgot to set an alarm for the most important day of my college career. I had spent the previous week sleeping in the freshman dorms for the "senior week" my college hosted for all the graduating seniors. This was the first night back in my comfortable queen bed, so as you can imagine, the sleep I found that night was one where it felt like I died and came back to life. Ironically, maybe this week reminded me of being a freshman a little too much.

Back then, I had also forgotten to set an alarm for the first day of NCAA compliance meetings for the equestrian team—one of the first tasks my coach (who made it clear she doesn't stand for people being late on the first day) assigned us. I sprinted there in my pajamas wearing a shirt that just so happened to say, "Sorry I'm so late" (an unintentional foreshadowing of the morning's events). I had no clue where I was going yet, so I banged on the door of our school cafe to ask the workers where the auditorium was. I finally found the right place and timidly sunk into my seat terrified my coach would cut me from the team before real tryouts even began. Luckily, she forgave me after my apology email promising to never be late again. I was so scared from that encounter that I was never, in fact, late again in all four years. This fear from freshman year was so instilled within my body that it found its internal alarm from the rain on the morning of my graduation. Since I realized I wasn't late, I calmed down and got ready as normal. I proudly slipped on my black graduation gown with my student-athlete sash and my study abroad in Ireland sash, excited to present to the world what I had accomplished these past four years.

Naturally, when most people picture the perfect day they picture one with bright blue skies and sunshine that beams so bright they have to squint their eyes. I always envisioned this for my graduation. I pictured standing outside the arena after the ceremony with all of my best friends taking photos and throwing our caps into the air to signify our success. Instead, I was met with nothing but torrential downpours the entirety of the day. We had to sprint into the arena praying our caps and gowns didn't get too soaked. Everyone was trying to avoid the rain, and the traffic was so bad afterward, that no one got to meet up with family or take photos. Although the day didn't go as I had pictured it would, I was still excited about the accomplishment of walking the stage on my college graduation. I had made peace with the weather happening on my special day, but I'd later realize that the rain held a lot more meaning than I ever would have imagined.

My graduation was considered to be a monumental and transitional day for me, a day when I graduated from being a student into a real adult. As everyone did, I held high expectations of what postgrad life would be like based on what I had seen and heard from friends and family who had already graduated. Therefore, I had hoped that this new adventure into adulthood would be one I could look forward to. To say the least, that impactful, rainy day that was my college graduation was certainly transitional, but it was into one of the rainiest seasons of my life.

I thought the summer after graduation would be filled with applying to exciting new jobs, and traveling to new cities in hopes I'd fall in love with one enough to move to and spend extra time with friends before our "big girl" jobs all began. Instead, I was glued to the bed in my childhood bedroom day after day watching the beautiful summer days pass by. I felt like I had fallen into a sticky spider web I couldn't get out of no matter how hard I tried. I wanted to get up and feel good, but I couldn't. I felt paralyzed emotionally, and it made me feel physically stuck. At first, I didn't understand what I was going through. I thought I was going through a weird, tired phase.

When I finally found some motivation to socialize, I vividly remember what it felt like when I arrived to visit my friends who were still living in our college house for one more year of grad school. I felt this deep feeling of what I can only describe as grief as I drove into my college town for the first time since graduation. That's when I realized I was dealing with some deeply heavy emotions that came from graduating. Emotions I was never prepared to feel and had no idea how to process as I'd never felt that way before. I felt silly as I knew I was privileged to go to college in the first place. I felt like no one else felt what I did and that my feelings weren't valid. People deal with so much worse, so why was I allowed to grieve my college life, right?

I was so wrong about this. What I didn't know was that I WAS valid in feeling these emotions. These feelings were very heavy to carry, especially as a young college grad who was supposed to feel ready to take on the world. I was dealing with what I now understand is called postgrad depression. A very real and common experience for graduates to go through, but one that was brushed under the rug and never discussed. As a kid and young adult, our identities are mostly decided for us. During college, I was used to responding to the question, "Tell me about yourself" with, "I'm a marketing major and an equestrian at Sacred Heart University."

I discovered through my own experience and after learning that others felt the same as me, that there is a big loss of identity young adults inevitably face when they are postgrad, whether it be from high school or college. Everyone mentioned job searches, salaries, marriage, and having kids after graduation. No one mentioned the in-between stuff during that journey where you have to start from scratch, relearning who you are as an adult, and deal with the emotions that go along with detaching from your childhood.

I was not ready to process the realization I had about the grief I was feeling deep down. The summer months continued to pass, and I watched my life go by as I accomplished nothing I thought I would. I had no inspiration or motivation, and my anxiety became out of control. I have dealt with anxiety since I was a kid, but it was manageable. I tried a job as a preschool teaching assistant thinking I would find a sense of purpose, or it would hopefully be what I wanted as a career. Nope, this made things so much worse. I now had the stress of helping to take care of fourteen three-year-olds, on top of the fact I hated the schedule, it wasn't for me. My anxious thoughts were now constantly spiraling out of control because as the months went by, the pressure to figure out my life increased. I felt like I had weights on my shoulders and after every month that went by, someone added more weight. The weight was becoming too heavy for me to hold, and my knees were buckling. My chest began to physically hurt from how fast my heart was beating due to the physical ways my anxiety was manifesting.

The moment when my life changed forever was one seemingly regular afternoon in the kitchen of the home I grew up in. I walked into the kitchen where both of my parents stood, and I began to sob. This was a big deal for me, as I had always been a little too independent and preferred to deal with my problems on my own. I hated burdening people with my emotions (which wasn't normal but was a can of worms I'd later open and process). At that moment, I reached my breaking point. The weight on my shoulders had finally become too heavy, and there was no way for me to carry it alone any longer. I cried to my parents about my anxiety and how I physically and mentally could not take it anymore. I finally opened up about how I had been feeling.

My parents supported me and were there for me in the best way they knew how, but it was more about the fact that I spoke out loud and admitted what I was facing. I felt empowered by this, and it took the weight off me in many ways. For the first time since before I graduated, I felt inspired to change my life. I went up to my room and picked up the book *The Secret*. This book details manifestation and the power of positive thinking, and it completely changed my life from that point on. Everyone has their ideas about the traditional Law of Attraction, but the manifestation aspect of the book wasn't what changed my life so immensely. The part that changed my life was learning about the power of our minds. As someone who dealt with constant spiraling, overthinking thoughts, I was a prisoner in my mind at the time. I didn't know I could live any differently. I thought some people had to struggle more in life than others. When I learned that my thoughts were in my control and I had the power to not only change my thoughts but use my thoughts to change my life, I was exhilarated.

Before this significant moment, I was so riddled with anxiety that I simply wanted a slice of stability. For a moment, I remember telling myself I could settle for making an average living in a regular old house in my hometown. The problem here was never about the amount of money or the house I envisioned; the problem was with the language I chose to say to myself. The word "settle" was a word that didn't fit who I was at all. I had always been someone who went after my biggest dreams. I stopped at nothing during high school to make it as an equestrian athlete who was deemed the underdog due to finances, and I succeeded! I had been rewarded with a scholarship as a student-athlete for four years of college.

That was who I was: someone who deeply cared about my dreams and would stop at nothing to achieve them. However, the pressures of postgrad life had swallowed me whole, and I lost touch with that version of myself. That led me to think settling was acceptable. I quiver at the thought of never having the breaking point I experienced and discovering mindset work. I would be an entirely different shell of

17

who I was meant to be had I never discovered what changed the direction of my life for good.

Suddenly, a whole new world opened up for me. I felt like the dreams that seemed out of reach were possible. I felt like I was finally going to change from feeling anxious all the time to feeling confident and peaceful. From that day on, I spent all my time researching mindset and implementing everything I learned into my life. My life was never the same, and changing my mindset changed the entire course of where my life was headed. I got a job as a nanny working only 30 hours a week with a schedule that was different every day, which I loved. I never liked doing the same thing every day. Having this job gave me the time and space to explore myself and start building a relationship with myself. There is nothing easy about taking care of kids, but something is healing about it. Kids remind you what life should be like, especially when you have the privilege of spending a ton of time with them every day.

I had what I would now name my aha moment when I began to see the evidence of how much changing my mindset changed my life. Changing my mindset allowed me to stop feeling the physical symptoms of anxiety (for the most part), learn how to stop my anxious thoughts in their tracks, create goals and a vision that represented my wildest dreams, and embody the qualities and emotions of the best version of myself. I realized this is what rewrote my narrative postgrad. I went from my story thus far being one where I struggled with depression, grief, and anxiety, and was moments away from settling for a life less than I deserved, to a story with a beautiful turnaround moment where I transformed despair into self-empowerment and success.

I knew I had to be there for other college graduates. I couldn't bear the thought of anyone else feeling alone with these heavy feelings. I began to start the conversation about the struggles of postgrad life online. I talked to teammates, friends, and even strangers on social media. I realized how although I felt so deeply alone, I was far from it. The only issue was no one was talking about it. Everyone was ashamed of going through it, so no one was speaking up. I decided to find the courage to speak up because I didn't want anyone else to go through the same struggles I did without any resources to get help. I remember when I was struggling, I Googled postgrad depression and found no resources, only career advice. I didn't need career advice, that was the last thing on my mind at that point. There were NO resources for getting your mental health on track postgrad and there were certainly no resources online warning people about the potential struggle with their mental health after college.

I decided this was going to be my life's work in some way or another. I knew I had stumbled upon and created something deeply valuable to society. I always knew I was meant to help people, but I never knew how I would end up doing it. This was how. I was meant to do this, and I knew it deep in my soul.

I had no idea how to start a business, or how I wanted to share my message with graduates. I just knew I had to begin. I started from scratch and brought what was a simple idea in my head into a real-life business. I began coaching people in their 20s for free on their mindset so I could gain experience doing what I wanted to do. I began helping people in my life. I started doing whatever I could do. No one in my family was a businessperson, so I was in the dark about how and what to do. I just kept going. Since I had a job that was only 30 hours a week and didn't overly stress me out, I had time to do all of this. I feel blessed that I allowed myself to admit that I hated the job as a preschool teacher and decided to try something a little more up my alley. Listening to myself and following my heart was always the key to my journey.

The period in my life I had all of these epiphanies was 2019 when I was 22, freshly out of college. Although this time lifted me out of a huge life funk and changed the direction my life was headed—the universe, God, or whatever you choose to call the higher power around us said, "Nope, you're not done learning, not even close." As it turned out, I would have my world within me crash again a year later, which changed my life even more than the first emotional crisis I went through. But we will get to that story. It will all tie together, and you will understand where all of this is coming from. I want to make it clear that it wasn't just one moment that caused me to never again struggle postgrad. Remember the sailboat I mentioned a few pages ago, the one that had to take on the six-foot waves and capsize that I wanted you to avoid? I was on that one. And even though I had moments where my boat sailed smoothly, the waters didn't fail to get rough again.

All of this, including the story I will tell you about later, led me to what I am doing today; writing this book, which talks minimally about career and mostly about how to deal with the difficulties of postgrad life. Writing a book was the exact answer to how I could get my message out into the world in a way that was accessible to ALL. The vast majority of people in their 20s who are postgraduates are known for having limited funds. I believe in my core that every single person deserves resources regardless of their finances, and writing this book was the perfect way to provide the resources that graduates need in the most affordable way possible.

Michelle Lynn Johnson

Making the active choice to change

Changing your life into one you love and have always dreamed of means you are going to need a little faith in yourself and this new process.

It's likely that if you have been actively trying to change your life for years and years with no luck, it has created the mentality in your mind that, "Nothing works. I'm just stuck like this." I understand what it feels like when you have applied yourself and gone out of your comfort zone to change, and you didn't get the results you hoped for.

Oftentimes, the reason you may not see changes in your life after applying yourself, is because you haven't consciously decided you are ready to change. There was still some resistance to the idea of your life becoming different than it is now, *even if* it meant it would change for the better.

If there is a part of us, deep down within, that doesn't feel ready to change or has too many attachments to our bullshit, we aren't going to see the changes we are looking for. Our mind will find a way to sabotage us from continuing because there is a belief hardwired within our brain that says this new change isn't safe. And if we don't know better, we will let our brain convince us to stop. We will listen to the excuses our mind feeds us.

You must actively *decide* you will do what it takes to become the best version of yourself. Say it with me. "I am ready to step into the best version of myself. I am brave enough to get uncomfortable and be honest with myself. I am ready to do what it takes to live a life I have always dreamed of."

Saying yes to this journey will inevitably come with difficult times. You must be willing to confront and face all the hard and painful situations and emotions that may arise during this journey. It takes true bravery to do this.

You are brave, though. I know you are. You are one of the people in this world who wants to be the best version of yourself. If you didn't, you wouldn't be reading this book.

The truth is, there is quite a small percentage of people in this world who are truly happy and are living a life they love and have always dreamed of. I'm sure you can guess why people settle for a life less than they want.

They don't want to face themselves. They don't want to feel uncomfortable. They don't want to feel painful emotions. They don't believe they are capable or worthy enough to live differently. They don't have anyone who ever taught them they can have more.

That is why I am so proud and excited you are here. I am honored to be the one to remind you of your worthiness and capability if no one has before. I am honored to show you the power of self-honesty and willingness to be brave in the face of heavy emotions.

If I never picked up a book about mindset and learned from my journey, I would never have known any of this either. I would have settled for a life that didn't light up my soul. I would have never met the best version of me or accomplished the dreams I was put on this Earth to accomplish.

There is great power in deciding to do things differently than you have in the past. One decision to fully embrace all of the newness that is to come, no matter how scary it feels, will change your life forever—in the BEST way. Your impact on this world will be magnificent, just by deciding to go all in on yourself. The energy of a person who lives authentically and shares their skills with the world to make it better leaves a mark.

Living a life you choose

The part of my story I shared with you about what I dealt with postgrad leads me to the first lesson I want to share with you. Why is it important to live a life you love and that **you** consciously created?

There are many scenarios where you may be pressured by other people to live a certain way. Maybe everyone in your family went to school to be a doctor, so you felt pressured to do the same. Maybe you do not resonate with the religion you grew up with anymore, but you feel pressured to abide by it because of family. Maybe it's the societal pressures to go to college, get a corporate job, get married, buy a house, and have kids. Whatever it may be, understand that *it is okay* to say no to these pressures if they do not align with what you truly want in your soul.

At the end of the day, **you** are the **only** person living your life. You are the only one feeling your emotions, living in the home you chose, living with the partner you chose, going to the job you're working, etc. Your choices need to align with what you truly want. The people who pressured you into these things aren't the ones who have to deal with the consequences.

It's difficult to upset people you love, there is no doubt about it. But, when you make decisions that align with your desires and what your soul truly wants, you're allowing yourself to become the most authentic version of yourself. When you wake up happy with the choices you made, you'll be able to show up as the best version of yourself in all aspects of your life. This is why I believe it's okay to disappoint people when you make decisions that align with your best self because people who *truly* love you and want the best for you will eventually adjust to the version of you that you *are*, not what they want you to be or think you are.

You deserve to live a life you are excited about every single day; every human being deserves this. You deserve to wake up and be proud of yourself for creating your life, no one else did it for you. It takes courage to do this. In your 20s, you need to find the strength within to find this courage. Your dreams and desires **do not lie** within the comfort of your current situation, they live right outside it.

Many people reach a point in their adulthood where they wake up and say to themselves, "Why can't I catch a break? Why can't I be happy? Why am I so exhausted with my life?"

They are confused about how their life turned out the way it did. But really, the reason isn't as complex as it may feel. The equation goes like this: Someone else choosing your life = a life outcome aligned with someone else's desires and not *your* unique desires.

I want to quickly (we will go into more detail in the second part of this book) introduce to you one of the most important concepts that will relate to everything you learn in this book, and I will continue to talk about it over and over again.

Your current reality is the sum of all the decisions you have made and the actions of your daily habits. The small choices you make might not seem impactful at the moment, but when you look back, you realize it was all of the small choices that brought you where you are now. Everything you think, feel and do consistently teaches your brain what to create more of in your future. If you are constantly doing things that create misery in your life, you will think thoughts that reflect that misery. When you think of thoughts of misery, you will continue to feel the emotion of it. A vicious cycle, but our brain is designed for consistency and familiarity.

When you live a life you are either complacent with or hate, the things you are doing daily are what drain your energy. If you aren't taking any actions aligned with your aspirations, you will inevitably feel burnt out and exhausted. *Life burnout is not the coincidence people think it is*, nor does it happen overnight. It is the outcome of consistently ignoring your wishes.

I learned this the hard way when I allowed myself to get complacent and too comfortable where I was. I think back to when I did the same thing every day, worked a job I enjoyed but didn't light a fire within me, and actively put my dreams on the back burner because I didn't know how to start following them.

Remaining in complacency and comfort would have been an easy route for me. I had skills in jobs that were deemed very valuable, I lived in a cute apartment with friends, and I paid my bills every month.

However, I was eventually met with this feeling of burnout. I was tired every day for "seemingly" no reason even though I slept more than enough, probably too much. I overdid it with caffeine. All I wanted to do was lay in bed and do nothing. I would

24

race to my bed after work and after socializing. This could have been considered normal or just part of life had I brought up this concern to anyone. Because, like I said, on paper I had it all together. I moved out, had a decent job I was good at, worked out and prioritized my physical health, and was very consistent emotionally (on the outside). I knew in my heart it wasn't how I was meant to feel or live, though.

I remember one car ride home to my apartment. I was feeling extra sad and realized I had honestly been lying to myself about how I had been feeling. I hated the word depressed because I had many family members who deeply struggled with it, and it didn't feel right or fair to say I was when I was functional day to day. I didn't have dark thoughts. I got up every day. I went to the gym five days a week. I still don't know if depressed was the right word for how I felt back then, but I know I was living in a way that was not right for me and I wasn't passionate or excited about life like I wanted to be.

I had been driving the car for my life, but it was becoming difficult to keep going because I was running out of gas. I was doing nothing to light up my soul or to pursue the dreams I had hidden away in my heart.

In no coincidence, right around the time I had that moment of self-honesty, I had an experience that caused me to never become complacent again. The car I was driving for my life finally ran out of gas, and I had to pull over. Metaphorically, I was stuck on the side of the road for quite some time before I learned how to fill it back up on my own. I'll explain later how I figured out how to "fill up my car" again.

This is a story I never thought I'd tell when it first happened to me because I felt crazy and thought I would sound crazy telling it.

I decided it was important to include it because it changed me forever in the best way possible, even though it didn't feel like that at first. It changed how I see myself, how I live, and how I feel about living. How could I leave out this key part of my story out of fear that some people may see it as weird?

So, with all of that being said, here's the story of my "spiritual awakening." I know there are a lot of you who will have no idea what that means or you might have some negative preconceived ideas about what it means. Just keep reading, you'll see that the term I am using has little importance in comparison to the story itself. It has nothing to do with organized religion and I am not pushing any sort of religious beliefs onto you, don't worry.

Michelle Lynn Johnson

My story is less about what I am naming the experience and more about what the experience taught me. If you are a human, you can likely relate to what I share, I just may call it something different than you would.

When I graduated from college in 2019, I felt this weird feeling deep in my soul on occasion. I hated the way it felt. I had thoughts like, "Even if I had all of the things I dream of what is the point of it all?" These thoughts took the enjoyment out of a lot of things and would creep up every time I started to find happiness in an activity, and I couldn't quite understand why.

I now name this feeling I experienced, "existential anxiety." It pretty much means exactly what it sounds like, I was anxious about what it means to exist. To put it another way, I was anxious about what it means to be human during this lifetime. I was confused about what it meant to live a meaningful and happy life because suddenly, what I was taught my entire life I should do to be happy and successful wasn't making sense anymore.

I couldn't understand the point of doing all the things we were told to do. I couldn't understand why so many people struggled to find happiness in adult life even after doing all the things. At the time, I wasn't ready to face these big feelings. I eventually shoved them so far away that I didn't feel them again for about a year.

Going back to that moment when I had to "pull over the car to my life", I believe this was *the* moment where my spiritual awakening began. I was now 23 and had JUST moved into an apartment with my two hometown best friends.

This apartment was only ten minutes from my parents' house, so it's not like I moved across the country. But those feelings of existential anxiety came creeping back in. Suddenly, my internal world seemed to crash within me. This feeling is really difficult to put into words. The only way I can explain it is that it felt like everything I knew about the world and what I wanted from it was abruptly ripped away from me.

Before this, I was comfortable and happy living my life as a 20-something having a good old time. I now felt like I wouldn't be able to experience life normally anymore because of how I felt and what I knew. It felt like the life path I was on and the person I was, was dying, and I had to let go of them and rebuild with the new "knowledge" I had. I had to grieve what I thought life was and who I thought I was going to be.

26

None of this was about anything I learned when I mentioned knowledge or "what I knew." Something *shifted* within my soul. I saw the world and myself differently. I saw people in a different light than I had before, but it was painful to realize. Now, when I listened to people talk, I could see their truth in a way. Like how sometimes people say things just to feel accepted, but you can tell they don't really feel that way in their heart. Or how you can see in someone's actions that they struggle to see their potential and worthiness. I was in turmoil over the fact that I realized most people in this world live a life that doesn't reflect their biggest dreams—that most people settle for much less than they deserve. I was in turmoil over the fact that most people, without realizing it, have deep-rooted fears that run their lives. The fears of not being enough, failing, being rejected, or being abandoned. I was in turmoil over the fact that I didn't know anyone else dealing with these huge existential crisis feelings.

This was before a lot of people went through this post-COVID (or at least started talking about it) and it became more normalized online.

I suddenly felt severely disconnected from everyone and everything happening around me. The worst part was that this was all so new to me, and I couldn't put anything I was feeling into words.

I was deeply homesick for something I couldn't put a finger on. Truly, it was the hardest thing I have ever gone through. I was lost on how to navigate it all. I didn't tell anyone except my mom, who also didn't understand but she *did* listen, and she didn't write me off.

I was lucky I only moved ten minutes away because I constantly slept at home in my childhood bedroom even though I just moved into my apartment. I needed some sense of comfort and normalcy. I had almost no social battery and didn't have the energy to socialize with my sweet roommates. They loved me through it and understood I needed to do what felt right for me at the time. I didn't tell them exactly what I was going through, but I expressed I felt weird emotionally and just needed time to myself to get through it. I was always lucky enough to have the best, most loving friends, and I feel so grateful I had them in my life during that time, even if I didn't open up about it.

The reality was that my external life wasn't going to stop even if I felt like it was stopping for my internal world. When you are struggling with emotional pain, I think it's natural to wish the world around you would pause for a little bit, so you have a minute to get up off your butt when you get rocked by life.

That being said, I continued to work every day like nothing was different. I was a nanny at the time, and even though my internal world felt like it was collapsing, I wouldn't have dared show that to the kids. I adored them. They were also adjusting to COVID life and needed stability since life was already crazy.

So, I went about my daily life portraying complete normalcy even though I felt weirder than I ever had. It was genuinely a "Jesus take the wheel" time in my life. I had no idea what was going on. I just kept going because I knew I couldn't do anything else.

I spent a lot of time lying in bed on my phone doing nothing productive and I understand now it was because I had no energy from all the emotional turmoil I was dealing with, along with the fact that I wanted to distract myself from what I was feeling inside.

As I mentioned, I felt like I was losing who I was in a sense. I felt like I wouldn't enjoy the things I had been doing, and I was scared to lose that part of me. I wanted to keep being young and clueless, it was much easier.

I kept going through the motions of my everyday life. This too shall pass I hoped, but honestly, I didn't know for sure if it would or if everything would be different going forward. I remember wishing I could go back to before I had this shift inside me. I would have traded it all for that at the time, even though I now see it as the best thing that has ever happened to me.

I call it my spiritual awakening because I resonated with all the characteristics of this type of awakening. When I googled the feelings I felt, this popped up and I felt my soul say, "Yup, this is what you are going through."

I don't remember exactly what I googled, I would imagine it was something like, "Why do I feel like nothing matters and I don't know what it means to be a human anymore." But I do wonder if it was some sort of divine reasoning I found the answers I did. Although I hated it at the moment because it was all too much, it did give me a sense of validation. I could talk online with people who felt what I did. I could make sense of it on some level, which I know if I hadn't I would have struggled a lot more for way longer.

An important detail of this whole story is that I live very internally. What I mean by that is I have a whole world going on within my mind, but on the outside, you'd have no idea what it's like inside my head. I am emotionally consistent. I don't have big reactions or emotional outbursts. I'm pretty collected in most situations.

28

Therefore, it would be hard for others to gauge what my internal experience is like without me outwardly telling them.

What I'm trying to say is, I'm very much the same person day to day, even on the bad ones. During this time of turmoil, it was completely internal. My external life didn't reflect it one bit. That was the craziest part; to be able to live so normally but feel so beyond normal.

I would meditate at night in my twin-sized bed in my old room because it helped me connect back with myself. During this time, I didn't feel so out of place in this world.

As I went through the days, read different books, and had different realizations about life I started to feel better and much more at ease. I began to see my spiritual experience as unique to me. I didn't need to be anyone specific; I didn't need to follow anything anyone else said as the truth unless it felt right, and I understood that everyone's spiritual experience is different.

I began to understand that I could no longer continue on the same path that resulted in the burnout I experienced if I wanted to live my full potential and purpose. I took a leap of faith and quit my job to pursue my dream of traveling the world, and I never looked back.

These realizations eased my mind about those fears I originally had that I would never be the same or enjoy any of the same things. I was able to understand I would always be me; I would just be wiser. It wouldn't make me less fun, less human, or less inclined to do the things I enjoyed as a 20-something.

I came to see spirituality and its effect on my life as simply my journey of growth and evolution as a human being. I learned to listen to my soul, my intuition. My soul knew best and as I evolved I knew what I needed, no one else held the answers for me. I knew what lessons I was learning during difficult times in my life, and I knew how to get myself through it. I trusted myself and my intuition as I practiced using it.

I learned what boundaries I needed to set, and as a former people pleaser, I taught myself the power of vulnerability and doing things even when I'm scared. I dared to confront my past, my wounds from childhood, and I stopped running from my emotions.

I was way too good at numbing myself with my phone or sleeping when I didn't want to feel things. I taught myself how to cry again because I very rarely let myself do this. I found the importance of feeling heavy emotions during my journey. I let myself have difficult conversations when I normally would have avoided confrontation at all costs. I taught myself that I didn't need to feel guilty when I set boundaries. I was extremely careful about who I let in my life after this, as I realized the past version of me wasn't as careful as I should have been. I learned so many lessons during this time of my life all based on *my* soul and what I was meant to learn to become who I am meant to be.

I'm grateful I learned to see my spiritual experience as this, instead of what I was scared it would be. I grew up religious, but this was different. Organized religion never resonated with me at a personal level when I was a kid, I participated because I thought it was the right thing to do. I always believed in a higher power, though. I was never an atheist by any means. My thoughts are that everyone is unique, and everyone will have beliefs that feel right to them. That is more than okay with me, I don't believe in deciding what is right or wrong in that area.

Throughout my 20s and since this unique turning point in my life, my spiritual experience has shaped me so much. I have grown immensely in ways I am proud of. I am proud of my character and the person I am. I am proud of how I treat people and the way I can hold space for anyone to be vulnerable, even strangers. I value human connection. I value the way a sense of community with other humans can provide so much peace, power, and happiness in life. I know all the skills I am naturally gifted with, and I have created my career and life because of it.

You deserve to live a life aligned with your inner dreams, just like I did. So, stick with me here, the difficulty of getting out of an old funk will subside, and getting into alignment will soon occur, I promise you this. I will show you how I was able to fill myself back up and drive the car of my life back onto the road.

This all taught me how much truth lies in the concept that everything in this life is happening for you, not to you. So, with that, let me unfold for you all the key perspective shifts and lessons that have changed my life over the years, and I truly believe they will change your life too.

The "in-between" stage

I've thought a lot about the solution to what almost everyone in their 20s goes through, what I call the infamous "in-between" stage. You're in between life stages where you were once a young adult, but you don't quite feel like a real adult yet.

You don't know where to live yet, because your hometown keeps you stuck, but the people in it keep you full. You want to find a new place, but the ache of starting over without your people is hard to cope with. Home is where the heart is, but it no longer feels like home. New places don't feel like home yet either. Sometimes, it's like you're homesick for a place you aren't sure exists at all.

You understand everyone else is also figuring it out, but it doesn't make it any less scary or confusing while you're going through it, because no matter what, you still feel like you should be doing more.

You want to take risks and travel and live your 20s, but you haven't gotten to a place in your career where you feel secure doing that. You don't want to miss out, but you also don't want to ruin your career for the sake of "you only live once."

You're navigating the transition from friendships that formed out of convenience, to friendships that last because of real effort, vulnerability, and connection. You realize it's up to you to decide which people are the ones you want to pour that effort into, but it's also scary recognizing some won't pour into you.

You're realizing that before this, you always had someone to tell you what to do next: teachers, coaches, your parents. You always had an outline for your life. Then you graduate and understand no one is coming to create your life for you. It's up to you. That transitional period is terrifying at first because everything is down to you making a choice.

And so I thought to myself—if only I could find the answer to this in-between period. The answer will solve everything for everyone.

31

I thought about it a lot. I logically thought about what processes and steps people could take to navigate this time. I came up with, literally, a whole book of processes and steps. But none of them will matter if you don't realize and truly understand this one important concept:

You will only be able to implement this roadmap for creating the life you desire and love once you *shift your standards* and your perspective on where you are now in life. It isn't defined only by logic. Here is the key; if you hate where you are in life and are stuck in the mindset of lack, you will have a difficult time getting started with any of this. You will give up on yourself before you even begin. You will assume and create the story in your mind that you're one of the people in the world who doesn't get to live an extraordinary life.

Here are the two things you need to do first before you get started on anything in this book:

1. Lean into this time of your life completely and accept where you are. You can't run from the person you currently are or where you are in your life. You have to start somewhere, and to begin, you must shift your perspective to say, "Okay, this is who and where I am right now in life. I'm okay with that. I accept myself exactly as I am. I don't need to be perfect and thriving all the time. This is a part of my journey."

2. Shift your standards for yourself. Before you try to do any of the work to change your life, you need to understand that your standards matter. *You are allowed to want extraordinary things, and you are worthy of having high standards for your life*. You are deserving of all the best things this world has to offer. At this moment, I want you to never lower your standards again out of convenience, out of being realistic, or out of low self-worth. Make the choice right now to *allow* yourself to have high standards in every area of your life.

Stop fighting what is. Stop hating where you are in life. Stop shaming yourself. You will **never** shame yourself into the life you want to live. You will never hate your way out of your hometown and current job. You will never hate yourself into a better you. The quicker you can release the resistance you have to your current situation, the smoother you will sail through.

The fact is your story and life path will unfold beautifully in the way that it's meant to. Getting through the mess that can be your 20s and this in-between period is what CREATES the unique life path you are meant to be on.

The mistakes you make, the times you feel depressed, the times you feel confused about what you are doing with your life, the times you lose friends, and the times you feel like you don't belong are all part of what you are meant to experience. There cannot be growth without experiences to grow from. You won't wake up tomorrow and be a completely different person because you did one mindset exercise in your journal.

Your growth and the creation of your dream life come from learning how to navigate through all the periods in your life, good and bad. Learning to create your dream life does not mean you are learning how to never experience difficult times. Instead, you are learning how to create a mindset that will allow you to gracefully flow through those difficult periods.

Your mindset will keep you grounded in the chaos that inevitably becomes our life sometimes. Your mindset will keep you from giving up on yourself and throwing in the towel on all of your hard work. Your mindset will push you out of bed on the days you feel like you can't keep going.

You do not want to reach the end of your 20s and realize you spent all of those years hating where you were. With acceptance of your circumstances will come freedom. Things will flow better for you once you accept that you are enough where you are now.

You deserve to let go of the heavy emotions that come with hating your current circumstances. It's time to let yourself be. Understand that although it may be messy, it IS part of the process. You're learning how to be an adult human for the first time, just like everyone else.

There is so much beauty in your current circumstances should you allow yourself to see it. There is beauty in everything. Allow yourself to find beauty in waking up to drink your morning coffee. Find beauty in crunching the leaves under your feet during your evening walk. Find beauty in listening to your friend talk about something they love. Find beauty in the fact that you can physically be around those you love while you can. Find beauty in taking care of a plant and watching it flourish.

There is no magic wand for this silly, messy period in between. It's okay to simply go through it all with no real idea what it'll be like on the other side. It's like driving through a storm. You might drive slowly, you might not be able to see which way to go and therefore the route is uncertain, or you might have to pull over and take a break. There's no right way to navigate it. But eventually, the storm passes, the route becomes clear again and you won't feel uncertain or worried anymore. You've entered a new, sunny day. You might feel like this season of your life is a bit like a storm, but I promise that acceptance of where you are in life and shifting your standards for yourself will allow you to come out on the other side and see that sunshine again.

Navigating the lows of life

I want to share the biggest lesson I learned throughout my 20s that completely changed my perspective on how I felt about life. This lesson may sound a little strange at first but stick with me.

Experiencing a "rock bottom" period in your life is *necessary* for you to reach new heights on your journey. Because of the way our thoughts naturally reflect our emotions, it's hard to see how anything good can come from our lowest moments in life. However, I assure you that your rock-bottom moments hold more importance than you realize.

You have probably heard the saying, "What goes up, must come down." That saying is true in life too, not just science. The truth is that life will have ups and downs. It's pretty much inevitable that your life will not be perfect all the time, and you will struggle sometimes.

I have learned to see life as a series of lessons placed for us to learn so we can grow and evolve as a human being. Each of us has a unique life path with different lessons to learn. Some of those lessons feel empowering, some we don't understand at first. Some we learn easily; some we need to face over and over again until we get the message.

The lessons with the most to teach us and allow us the most growth will be the ones that feel the most uncomfortable. These lessons may require you to feel heavy emotions, go through difficult situations, and overall feel like you hit your personal rock bottom.

In those moments, without this knowledge that the difficult time you are going through is simply a lesson needed for you to grow, you may feel like it's the end of the world. You may struggle to deal with the heavy emotions that come with this challenging time. You may feel like it is never going to get better.

Before I go on, I want to make it clear that life events, such as the passing of a loved one or something traumatic you may have gone through, do not need to be intellectualized into a life lesson. I recognize it can be deeply frustrating to hear someone tell you "everything happens for a reason" regarding your trauma. The difficult times I am referring to are periods of your life you consider to be "dark" moments or "stuck" moments within your personal growth. However, know the message of "this too shall pass" absolutely applies to any trauma. You can and will eventually feel better no matter what you have gone through.

Learning the significance behind life's hardships will allow you to flow through it much more easily. A rainy season of your life will no longer feel like it will be raining forever, you'll know with certainty the sun is on its way.

Think about it this way. Let's say you have the goal to be a successful, confident leader who runs your own business someday. Currently, you may have insecurities blocking you from becoming your most confident self. To become this confident version of yourself, you will have to work through your insecurities.

For you to work through these insecurities, you need to become aware of them. Lessons can show up in your life in many different ways. For instance, a person may show up in your life who triggers those insecurities and brings them to the surface. This person may, for example, make you feel "not good enough." This insecurity is one you likely already held inside, but that person triggered you in a way making it obvious that you weren't as confident as you thought.

On the surface, if you don't know how to look for the lesson in this negative situation, you will simply see it as that "bad person" who made you feel horrible. You will allow yourself a pity party of, "I always meet the worst people and life isn't fair to me." This isn't to invalidate that the person very well may have been terrible, but the experience of not feeling good enough isn't about them. It's about the part of you that didn't feel good enough already, and this person triggered this belief you already held. Sometimes, people are like mirrors. They show us what we judge in ourselves, our insecurities, and our fears.

This experience may last the entirety of a relationship —months or years even. During this experience, all of your insecurities were brought to light. After the relationship ends, you're left at rock bottom, feeling the worst you have ever felt with not an ounce of confidence left. You will probably feel quite stagnant and stuck in your life. You may not be very productive and feel lazier than usual.

The lesson here is this experience allowed you to see all of your insecurities for what they are, right there to grab and process. This stagnant time is there for you to heal and shed your old layers. It's there for you to take extra time and rest after you

36

work through these insecurities and heavy emotions. Processing difficult emotions and shedding old layers takes a lot of energy. You may need more rest than usual and are not lazy to need it.

Without knowing this lesson, you may feel like a failure. You may feel like you keep running into stagnant, stuck periods in your life and you can't figure out why. You may keep having these periods over and over again, because there's a lesson the universe is begging you to learn, but you haven't gotten the message yet.

Not to sound cliche, but it's like when a caterpillar becomes a butterfly. The caterpillar goes into a cocoon and evolves into a beautiful butterfly. During the time it was in its cocoon, the butterfly was resting and appeared stuck—just like how you may feel during your difficult time. The thing is, though, the butterfly was never actually stuck. When a caterpillar goes into its cocoon, it completely dissolves and *rebuilds* into a butterfly. This time of rest was imperative for the caterpillar to be able to rebuild into its next, more evolved version of itself. Feeling stuck and resting more during difficult periods of life does not equate to a lack of growth or progress.

When I went through times like these, I felt frustrated and upset. I felt stuck and like nothing good ever happened to me. I was sick of the difficult times, and I simply couldn't understand why this was happening so often.

Until I learned the lesson. I realized I had huge goals for myself and an ideal version of who I wanted to be in this life, and somehow I had to get there. I wasn't going to get there overnight by wishing. I was going to get there by going on this life journey of learning about myself in the form of lessons so I could grow into the person I was meant to be.

So now, I recognize that when life isn't going so well or when I feel stuck, I see it's because I have some growing to do. I have to go in my "cocoon" for a while so I can come out a better version of myself. And that's just that.

The difficult times will be much easier to get through when you see why they are there. You won't feel like you're failing or there is something wrong with you. You will see it is all part of your journey, and it's not a bad thing after all. You will see you emerge better every time, and that you ALWAYS come out of it. The difficult times always end.

The good part is, no matter how well people hide it, everyone is doing the same thing you are on their journey of life. Although unique to the individual, everyone experiences the highs and lows of life. Everyone experiences heavy emotions.

Everyone has to learn lessons, even though many people will choose to close their eyes in the face of a lesson they could learn (you know the people who do this).

If you choose to be brave and speak about your hardships, I bet you'd find a connection with those around you over the humanness you all share. We don't have as many original experiences as we may think we do in this life.

Feeling difficult emotions

Feeling difficult, heavy emotions is part of being human. As we discussed, there will always be periods in our lives where we don't feel our best. Humans feel a large spectrum of emotions: joy, bliss, passion, excitement, and gratitude. We also feel more difficult emotions such as anger, frustration, grief, anxiety, depression, or numbness.

When we experience these heavy emotions, it's common to not know how to properly process and deal with them. A person may react intensely when experiencing these emotions. People who consistently have intense emotional reactions are what I like to call "reactive."

This essentially means that in the face of an inconvenience that causes an emotion such as frustration or anger, the person has a highly emotional reaction. Instead of processing the emotion, they have an outburst.

Let's use an example to make sense of what this could mean in everyday life (and this is one I have witnessed many times as a traveler). Let's say you're on board your flight to leave for your destination, and the flight attendant announces there's an issue with the aircraft and the flight will be delayed.

A reactive person is going to make a huge deal and throw a fit. You know exactly the person I'm referring to if you have been in this situation before. They won't be able to effectively process this feeling of frustration, so they will throw their hands up in anger stating, "This is ridiculous!" They may pick a fight with the flight attendant and demand someone fix the problem.

Here's the thing, this situation is out of everyone's control. The pilot, the flight attendant, and the other passengers have no control over the delay. When something is out of everyone's control, the appropriate reaction is to remain calm even if they feel frustrated. When someone knows how to properly cope with difficult emotions such as frustration, they can remain patient in the face of inconvenience. A reactive person who cannot properly cope will have big outbursts.

Another situation that can happen when someone without proper emotional coping skills feels a difficult emotion, is that they want to get rid of these feelings as quickly as possible. In today's world, it's easier than ever to do so. If someone is experiencing any type of heavy emotion, they can distract themselves. Everyone is quick to run out for a drink after a hard day of work, or mindlessly scroll on social media for hours during a breakup. It's *easy* to avoid heavy emotions when we have those types of activities to numb ourselves from feeling. Most of us have done this at some point, whether we realize it or not. I know I have!

People may opt to distract themselves from the heavy feelings, so they never have to fully feel or process them at all. Or they may focus on the heavy feelings *so much* that the feelings grow even bigger than they were to begin with. What you focus on will expand. And yes, it's no myth, the more you focus on how bad you feel, the worse you will continue to feel.

Learning about processing heavy emotions was one of the most impactful lessons I had to learn. This was a lesson that reminded me that if I wanted to be the best version of myself, I had to be willing to do hard things. Avoidant behaviors are the easiest option—but it is the route that keeps you the same.

Everyone learns how to process emotions differently due to how their parents taught them or *didn't* teach them. If you currently are a reactive person, a "focus on the negative" person, or a numb-out person, don't beat yourself up! Most of us are one or all of these at some point.

Remember, our journey of life is designed for learning. We don't come to Earth with all the answers, and we are all doing our best with the information we have at the moment.

I didn't process my emotions at all. I was very good at numbing myself with distractions like my phone or sleep to avoid negative emotions. I used to think it was a good thing that I barely ever cried. I had to get honest with myself and come to terms with the fact that it was unhealthy for me to ignore my emotions and never truly process them. I quite literally had to re-teach myself how to feel those heavy emotions. This meant letting myself cry when I needed to, even if it meant I had to take myself on car rides and listen to sad music to release the pent-up emotions inside.

Give yourself the gift of feeling. This will help you understand yourself better, show up in your relationships better, and overall feel more connected with yourself.

This will help you be an emotionally mature adult who can deal with inconveniences without shutting down. This is something we all have to learn how to do, it just depends if and when a person learns it.

Ideally, a parent teaches this to their child at a young age: teaching them to take deep breaths when they are upset, teaching them to communicate when they are upset without yelling, teaching them that it's okay to feel "big" emotions and that it's okay to cry or get angry as long as it is expressed in a way that isn't harmful to themselves or others.

However, not every parent *knows* how to teach this. It is likely because their parents didn't know how to teach them either—not knowing how to process emotions is something that is often generationally passed down. This is why many kids grow up to be adults who have the emotional maturity of a child. Not everyone will learn this, some people will go their entire lives never learning how to process emotions healthily.

Part of this journey of building a relationship with yourself will include getting in touch with your emotions. You can begin this now by taking the time to become aware of how you currently process emotions. The next time you feel angry, I want you to notice how you naturally cope. Do you lash out at others? Do you make sure everyone in your path feels your wrath? Do you retreat to your bedroom? Do you drink it away?

Your homework for this lesson is to work on your awareness of your emotions and your reactions to them. For now, that is all it needs to be. Start getting in touch with how you feel and begin getting to know your current coping mechanisms. Are you an emotion avoider? Are you already in touch with how you feel?

This is one of the pieces to the puzzle of relearning yourself in your 20s. Getting in tune with your emotions and learning how to properly cope when things get hard is the beginning of building your emotional maturity.

Your relationship with yourself, and others, and your ability to navigate through the world will drastically improve just from creating awareness of how you currently operate.

Michelle Lynn Johnson

Building emotional maturity

Perspective shifts are the simplest way to make big changes. Sometimes, all it takes is *deciding* to see the world from a new perspective. Remember: the same actions = the same results. The same goes for your way of thinking. Changing the way you see things will change the way you feel.

I wanted to share with you some perspectives I have learned throughout my journey that helped me develop my emotional maturity:

People *will* have different opinions than you. This doesn't always mean you have to cut the person off immediately, fight back to get them to agree with you, or remain closed off and not get to know other parts of them. It's natural that not everyone will agree with your opinions and that you won't agree with theirs. However, building tolerance for other people's differences will help you be emotionally mature in relationships with others. If you shut down and close off at the first sight of disagreement, you may lose the opportunity to connect with people. That person who you may have one different opinion from may have ten more opinions you both agree on, and they could be an amazing person. Unless this truly bothers you from a moral standpoint, it's helpful to remain tolerant and open to others who have different opinions from you so you can get to know the other parts of them that you may love.

Consider what you have control over in each situation. If you are faced with a frustrating situation, it can be easier to focus on the negative. Focusing on the parts you have no control over will not help you fix the situation. It will make those difficult emotions grow and you will feel worse. Take a deep breath and consider what you can do to make the situation better. Sometimes the only thing you can do is ride out the difficult emotion until it passes, and it always does. Try to remain patient with yourself and others. This takes practice, but the more you do it, the calmer you will be in the face of inconvenience.

If you're dealing with heavy emotions that you are struggling to work through, try a few of these techniques to learn to cope and process. A great way to process and understand your emotions is to journal. Do a "brain dump" where you write out everything inside your mind you are thinking and feeling. Try to get to the root of why you are feeling this way and what may have triggered these thoughts and feelings. Over time, you can look back in your journal and find the patterns within your thoughts and emotions to help you better understand yourself. This can help you make sense of what you are going through.

Another way to process heavy emotions is to ask a trusted friend or a professional to help you navigate what you are feeling. It can be helpful to express your feelings out loud and get another perspective to see things differently. Sometimes, it can be difficult to understand what you are feeling when it is stuck inside of your head. Spiraling thoughts can confuse you and take you down many different rabbit holes, so writing down what you feel or speaking to someone else can help you get a better understanding of what you feel.

Create a safe space for yourself to feel your emotions. For me, the car is a safe space. Whatever it may be for you, find a place that feels comfortable for you to release your emotions. Crying allows you to release those bottled-up feelings, and you will feel better afterward! So many people see crying as a sign of weakness. I encourage you to see it as healing, and that you are doing your body a favor. Many of us, especially men, are taught not to cry. "Don't be a baby, man up!" Crying is such a natural way to release emotions, and when we don't allow ourselves the opportunity, these emotions stick around within our bodies. Sadness evolves into anger when it's ignored. The angriest people you know have probably swallowed their need to cry and their pain so many times that it turned into rage. If you aren't used to allowing yourself to feel and cry it out, this may feel uncomfortable at first. That's okay. Remind yourself it's okay and it is **safe** to feel! Understand these emotions will eventually pass, they always do. Allow them fully. Acknowledge them fully. Accept them fully. Experience what they feel like in your body. Listen to what thoughts come up in your mind when these feelings arise. Get familiar with what happens when difficult emotions arise, this is another part of getting to know yourself on a deeper level and creating a stronger relationship with yourself. Close your eyes and breathe through the difficult feelings and thoughts, reminding yourself these emotions are part of being human.

When it comes to relationships with others, another part of becoming emotionally mature is learning how to deal with other people's emotions. When other people you love are feeling difficult emotions, there are a few things that may happen to you. You may feel uncomfortable with their emotions and not know how to be there for them, so you may be dismissive or avoidant. You may also feel like their heavy emotions are your fault or your responsibility to fix, so you may take it personally if someone you love is having a bad day. Like everything else, this will take time to learn. You may feel uneasy at first, and that's normal and okay.

One of the most important ways to be there for someone emotionally is to actively listen and hear them fully. Most of the time, people want to feel heard and validated. They want to know that someone understands what they are feeling and going through. Even if you don't know how to comfort them or fix what they are feeling, a simple "I hear you and I'm here to support you through this," can be enough to help someone feel a little better, and a little less alone. If someone is expressing that something you did upset them, this can be very triggering to the individual at fault. Immediately, the defense comes out. You may want to jump to defend your actions and explain why you are innocent in the situation. The fact is, even if what you said or did was unintentional, that doesn't mean the person shouldn't feel their emotions. The key here is to first listen to the person you have upset and try your best to understand their perspective. Remember, you don't have to agree with their perspective, but it is important to try to see why they feel the way they do. Again, validating that you understand where they are coming from, and that you hear them can go a long way. In relationships, both with friends and romantically, you will inevitably upset the other person at some point whether you mean to or not. Learning to appropriately respond in conflict will help you build strong, long-term relationships.

Michelle Lynn Johnson

Relationships in your 20s

Your relationships will change a lot in your 20s, especially after graduation. This is because our lives are going through big changes, both in our environments and new lifestyles. We are no longer right down the hall from our friends and friendship is no longer as convenient.

The biggest piece of advice I have for you when it comes to relationships in your 20s is to be open to your relationships changing. Try not to cling on for dear life to what once was. What once was will likely not remain as you get older, and that's okay!

The people who stay in your life in your 20s should be people you can see yourself growing with as you get older. You will change so much every year after you graduate from college, and your needs and desires change as well.

Relationships with people who want you to stay the same as you always were, typically have no intentions of growing themselves and will hold you back.

You will have to "re-introduce" yourself to some people and show them who you are now as you have grown. This might mean reminding people of the behaviors you no longer partake in, showing them the ways that your personality has evolved, and sharing your new interests. Especially if you have friends or family members you don't see very often.

Friendship and your relationship with your family members become a choice. You are no longer forced to go to family events or sit next to your friend every day in class. These relationships will require effort. They will require you to show up for people even when you are tired from work, but your friend is struggling that day. They will require you to spend your extra saved money on plane tickets to visit your best friend who lives in another state. They will require you to pick up the phone and check in with your sibling who you no longer live with to make sure they are doing okay. Relationships become a choice, and they require your effort, even when it's not easy. Decide who is worth pouring into and pour into them. The right people will pour back into you, and the wrong people won't. You will see clearly who they are.

When you find your people, cherish them. Show up for them during their low points even when they aren't able to show up for you temporarily. Love them without expecting anything in return. Show them grace when they are going through busy periods and can't pick up the phone as often as they used to, or they can't visit as much as you would like. When you are lucky enough to find people worth keeping in your life as adults, it is always worth investing in them.

This also goes for romantic relationships. If you meet someone in your 20s who you feel you could see yourself having a future with, make sure they are someone you can grow with. Someone who will be open to the person you evolve into as you get older, and who wants to continuously grow and evolve themselves. The person you are in your early 20s will likely be very different from the person you are when you are in your late 20s. You will grow to have new hopes and dreams, you will develop more security within yourself, and your personality might evolve. The right person for you will be open to your changes. They won't throw it in your face and remind you, "You've changed. I don't know you anymore." They will happily get to know every version of you. They will celebrate your evolution into an even better version of yourself. And you will equally celebrate theirs.

On the other hand, if you *don't* meet a romantic partner in your 20s, it's very common for people to feel behind. I want to help you change your perspective on this. Currently, you feel behind because of what is normalized in society. What has been normalized for years and years is for people to get married and have kids in their early to mid-20s.

This causes young adults to feel pressured to do the same. However, you can't put a timeline on finding love. Love is not something you can force and look for endlessly. The more you seek it out with chaotic, "time is ticking" energy, the more likely you are to settle with the wrong person. This is because you're looking for love from a place of *need*. You are more likely to convince yourself someone is right for you when they aren't and overlook red flags.

Due to the pressure society places on people to follow the classic timeline: college, marriage, house, kids, retirement—people feel like they are doing something wrong if that timeline doesn't seem to happen for them. They feel attached to this timeline because it's how they pictured their life would go from a very young age.

We are all unique individuals born into this world with different needs, desires, and interests. How can we all be expected to follow the same sequence of events in our lives that are molded for only one type of person, when we are all so unique?

Many people know in their souls that this path isn't what they want, but they are so attached to it that they have trouble accepting they want something different.

Take your time. Allow life to flow as it's meant to, without trying to control the outcome. Tuning out the noise from other people won't be easy, but it *will* be worth it.

Your life will be perfectly crafted in the imperfections that are your journey. The mistakes, the failures, the breakups, the times you gave too many chances, all of it. Your path is not meant to be a perfect series of events where you know each move you will make and how to make it. All of it is unknown for a reason. We have to relinquish the death grip we have on the need to control every little detail and the need to create perfection in our lives. These are two of the most impossible standards we can set for our lives.

No life path is better than the other, it **only** has to do with your unique desires and where you are in your life right now. Wherever you are in your life, there is a perspective shift that will allow you to see the beauty in where you are if you choose to see it.

I am pleading with you to please stop beating yourself up for where you are in your life. There is no such thing as being behind, only the invisible pressures from society and the people around you cause you to feel behind. I will say this over and over throughout this book, **find the courage to follow your desires**. This is your life. No one else except for you knows what will make you happy in your lifetime.

Michelle Lynn Johnson

Developing patience for the unknown

Throughout the entire course of your life, you will need to learn to be patient, especially in your 20s. There are many times in your life when you will find yourself wanting to wait for a certain outcome. You might wonder to yourself, "Well, when is it my turn?" You might watch everyone around you get what you want but you don't have it yet. You might have worked harder than everyone else, but you still don't have it. This is an incredibly natural thing to go through. Everyone has done this, I have too.

However, these feelings of frustration and resistance come from our attachment to certain outcomes. You have expectations and desires you create within your mind, and when you don't achieve them, self-criticism begins.

You are attached to the idea that things have to play out how you decide they must. It is vital to realize and understand that life doesn't always play out in the exact timeline you originally decided it needed to. A lot of the time we think we know what we want or what would be best for us at that moment. But in all honesty, we don't always know.

I want you to consider a time in your life when you hoped, prayed, and begged whoever you believed in for something you wanted to happen. Maybe you were dying to get a certain job that seemed perfect for you. At that moment, you attached yourself to the idea that this was the only outcome for you. This is what was right for you. But months go by, and you don't get the job. You are crushed and can't believe, "Once again, you didn't get what you wanted."

You want to create the narrative in your mind that nothing ever works out for you when things like that happen. You want to wallow in self-pity and believe you never get what you want.

As time went on, you ended up landing a pretty good job. Yet you aren't as excited about it as you were about the other one. That is until you see *why* you were never meant to get the other job and why you *were* meant to get this one.

51

One day during your lunch break you walk to a local cafe. You're sitting down alone at a table until a really cute person sits down with you and sparks up a conversation. They end up being the love of your life. And you met them because you took the second job after not getting the first.

At the moment, we think we have the answers to exactly what will make us happy. And in a sense, we do. But the key to remember is when we don't get what we want in the time frame we expect it, it's because there is a better plan in store for us.

I love the quote, "If not this, then better." I say this to myself when I want something to happen in my life. I'm never afraid to ask the universe for what I want, but I don't attach myself to the outcome. I have learned from experience that when I don't get what I asked for, it's because there is something even better in store for me, should I be open enough to see it.

I do not allow myself to wallow in the emotion of, "I never get what I want." It holds no truth, and I will not allow it to have any power over me. That statement and the emotions that come with it do not help you get what you want, they hold you back and keep you stuck in the feeling of what you lack. I always get what I *need*, which is what matters. I trust there is a higher power in this world that knows what I need, and this matters more than what I think I want. There are countless times this has proven to be true in my life. Many times I have said to myself, "Well, good thing that didn't happen." More than I can count.

I'll share with you one of my favorite examples of this happening in my life. Right after I graduated and moved back home, I had no idea what I wanted to do for a career.

Suddenly, I *thought* I had the perfect idea. I decided I wanted to be a teacher. I had always loved kids and knew it in my soul. Therefore, I thought diving into becoming a teacher would be the answer to the part of me that felt a lack of control and stability in my life.

This was crazy considering I had *just* graduated with a marketing degree. But I was always an all-or-nothing kind of girl and wanted to go for it. I remember looking into different grad school programs and nearly applied to a few.

Eventually—and I'm very glad I went this route—I decided to start as a teaching assistant at a preschool to see if I liked it. I quickly realized I hated it. After only three weeks, I knew an 8-5 schedule was never going to work for me. I am too free-spirited for that strict of a routine. I quit as soon as I understood this.

At that time I knew I wanted to work with kids, but it wasn't how I thought I should. I was attached to the idea that I needed a routine day job like everyone else, it felt like the only acceptable option at the time.

I came to learn I was meant to be a nanny instead. I was meant to nurture only a few kids, rather than 14 in a classroom. The nanny job gave me the time and space to figure out what I wanted to do: own a business helping people live their dreams.

Although I was intent on the idea of becoming a teacher, I was thankful I never went back to school. But it wasn't all for nothing. Every decision I made during that time was meant to happen. The 8-5 teaching job showed me what I didn't want to do, while the nanny job gave me the flexibility and time to learn what I did. If I had gotten what I wanted initially, I would have become a teacher and spent a lot of time and money to realize I didn't want to do it.

There were many moments after this, which felt truly meant to be. For instance, when I started my coaching business, I met a girl I was meant to meet. She and I were exactly alike. Her life was similar to mine in many ways. I had never found insane similarities with another person, and they weren't just coincidence.

We grew up in comparable ways. We were born the same year, only two days apart, our personalities were like mirrors of each other, we shared many of the same life struggles, and it felt like we had known each other all our lives.

The reason I met her was even crazier. I made a TikTok asking for volunteers to help me start my business and gain experience mentoring.

I received hundreds of responses in my email, one being from her best friend who found my video. I didn't see her friend's email, but I saw hers. Out of all those emails, hers stood out to me.

We knew it wasn't a coincidence that I chose to work with her, and we had all of those crazy synchronicities. We decided to keep being friends and ended up traveling together. I flew to her family's home in San Diego (we grew up across the country from each other) and it was like we knew each other our whole lives.

We flew to Hawaii where we planned to volunteer and work for a month. That didn't go exactly how we expected and is a crazy story for another time. Instead, we spent 16 days together, every day all day. Her friends whom we stayed with thought we had been friends beforehand and were surprised when we told them it was our first time meeting in person.

Had I never made that video, had her friend never seen it and sent it to her, had I never seen her email, I never would have met her.

I am sharing this with you so you can understand the reasoning behind the need to be patient with what is meant to unfold for you on your path. Things will work out in mysterious ways and amazing things can happen from *one* singular choice, but these beautiful things life will offer will sometimes require your patience and openness.

There will be occasions when things unfold at the time you want them to. Plenty actually. Life isn't just a series of disappointments, I promise you.

But it's the times in life when you are left begging and pleading to a higher power to please make it happen for you, and when it doesn't, will be when you need to understand this.

You always have a choice to see the glass half empty or half full. You have the choice to dwell on what is *not* happening for you or to trust the process.

This simple shift in perspective will change how you see your life going forward. When you understand there is a reason behind the delay in what you are wishing for, you won't torture yourself over why it hasn't happened yet.

Think of it like watching a movie you've never seen. It can be irritating not knowing what will happen next, and you get all worked up about it waiting for the outcome.

You might find yourself yelling at the screen because you couldn't believe why a character would make such a dumb decision. It riles you up and gets you so frustrated, you want to turn it off. But a few scenes later, you see why the character did it and everything begins to make sense.

Many times, this is how life is. You get frustrated with how things are playing out and want to throw in the towel and give up. But when you don't give up, you will see the resolution and why you went through that crazy time when many things were left unanswered. And when watching a movie, you CAN turn it off and make the early decision to hate the movie (give up) or you can watch it play out and choose to see the good parts (allow yourself to see why it worked out differently than you wanted it to).

Patience and faith take practice like anything else. This is part of building the relationship with yourself that I keep mentioning. When you practice enough, you will reach a point where you are naturally calm and at ease about the future. You will develop an inner knowing that what is meant for you will never pass you by. It eases the need to control every outcome.

I'm a dreamer and a visualizer, so I dream about very specific things I want in my future. It's exciting for me and gives me something to work for and look forward to. But as much as I dream of all the things I would love; I am perfectly okay with my path looking different than I thought it would. I know if what I asked for is meant for me, then I will have it. If I don't, it was never meant to be mine. It is as simple as that. But it won't feel simple until you practice the art of having faith and trust.

So, now you know how to get through uncertain times in your life. But you may *still* feel you are behind, and this makes it hard to detach from the very specific outcomes you are hoping for. Feeling this way is very common.

I hope to change your perspective and thoughts on feeling behind. Although these feelings are normal to experience because of the culture in our world, they shouldn't be normalized. You deserve to feel good about where you are, no matter where you are on your journey.

Michelle Lynn Johnson

Why it's okay to not know what's next

Be courageous enough to not know what is coming next in your future. As a student and a kid, you know what's next to come. You have another semester of school planned out for you, and what you'll be doing a year from now while you're in school.

A lot of people in their 20s freak out when they no longer have their next steps planned out for them. Suddenly, it's up to them to decide what is next. Losing the security that comes with being a student is terrifying, there's no doubt about it.

I want you to try your hardest to find within yourself the courage to *decide* it's okay not to know. When it comes to feeling better, becoming the person you want to be, and changing your life completely—everything starts with *just one* decision. Believe it or not, your life is made up of all the little decisions you made throughout your entire life. One little decision can change everything. I mentioned in the last lesson how one decision can be the door to meeting the love of your life, your best friend, or discovering your purpose.

Changing doesn't have to be this big, drastic, and overwhelming event. Change can and will come from all the times you make little decisions to shift your perspective and open your mind to seeing life in a new way. It's the decision to become an optimist within a world where you can easily choose to see the bad rather than the good.

Let it start with little decisions. I encouraged you to decide to be patient with the timeline meant for you, and now I want you to make another small decision. Have the courage for things to be unknown for a little while. The same, but there are more concepts I want to share with you to help it all hit home.

The sudden terrifying feeling of no longer having anyone holding your hand in life is why it takes courage to decide to let things be unknown. Terrifying, yes. But there can be two truths at once. The other truth is that it's a gift to have a blank slate to create your life as you want it to be.

You are freer than ever when you have no one else to consider when making decisions about your future. The world is your oyster! You are *not behind*, you are free.

I assure you that when you are living authentically, focusing each day on your *now*, you can trust that whatever unfolds in your future is aligned with the best version of you.

Even though you don't know what your future will look like a year from now, you can find peace in knowing the person you are working to become in the present moment is creating a life you will be so proud of in the future. Remember, your future is just the sum of all the little decisions you make now.

You're doing the work. You're taking the steps. You are doing your best with what you know. Inevitably, it will unfold how it is supposed to. I think a lot of people get overwhelmed in this part of their life because they think it's the end of the world if they make the wrong choice.

They think if they take the wrong job, commit to the wrong person, move to the wrong city, or spend too much time feeling stuck that they are ruining their future.

I don't believe in wrong decisions. I know this sounds ridiculous. Stick with me. I **don't** mean there are no wrong decisions when it comes to moral dilemmas, because truthfully, if you consistently make morally wrong decisions no one can defend or rationalize that.

What I am, however, referring to are the decisions you make in daily life. Like whether you should give someone another chance, book that trip, take a new job, move to a new city, or say yes to an opportunity. I know these are the very things that occupy so many of your minds right now.

No matter what you decide when it comes to issues like those, there isn't a wrong decision. I'll lay it all out for you, so you see what I mean.

Maybe you signed a lease in a new city, and you hate it. I bet it feels like the end of the world. Maybe this causes you to spend a lot of time at home. You feel devastated and shame yourself for making that decision. "Why would I ever come here? Who am I to think I can handle such a big change alone? I just ruined everything."

The way I see it, during this time you may not be living your best life or feeling many feel-good emotions, but you're still growing in a way that will benefit you more than you think.

You're learning how to deal with loneliness, you're learning how to navigate sadness without direct support from friends and family, or maybe you need a little extra time alone to rest and heal before your next big adventure.

This decision didn't ruin your life, it just added a different twist to your path. You will still be on the same journey at the end of the day, you just took a different turn along the way.

It is *safe* to make mistakes. It is safe to embrace the possibility that you might feel a mess at times. It is safe to start over if you need to. None of this means you are a failure, not good enough, or falling behind.

Sometimes it's the very decisions that feel "wrong" and catapult us into these messy periods of our lives, which are the ones that teach us things we need to learn to prepare us for our next chapter. This is why it's so important to decide to remain faithful and trust your life will always, no matter what decision you make, unfold how it is meant to.

Do not become crippled by the weight of making decisions during this time of your life. Boldly listen to your gut and allow yourself to decide without wondering endlessly if it is the right choice. Do not spend forever trying to decide. You know from the moment you had the idea what was the right thing to do, but your brain will always give you a hundred reasons why it's wrong if you let it.

Hopefully, by now you can see a reason to take the pressure off of yourself and take a much-needed breath.

The second part of this lesson, "Why it's okay to not know what is next," is about the emotions that often come with not knowing.

I already know that if you're someone who doesn't know what you want to do in your adult life, you have shamed yourself endlessly for it. You are relentlessly telling yourself you are behind, you are less than other people who have it figured out, and you are failing as an adult.

The next little decision for you to make is to let go of the shame you are carrying. Remember, this will create a great impact. There is no reality where shaming yourself has led to anything productive or helpful.

I want to let you in on a little secret I learned from traveling and speaking to countless older adults. No one has figured it out completely. I don't think anyone ever reaches a certain age and feels like they have suddenly mastered life. My grandmother, who is in her 80s, says she still feels like a teenager in her mind at times.

Life is an ever-changing journey that can never be entirely predicted or assumed. Everyone will deal with stress, worry, confusion, and pain throughout it. It is possible that if you have your career figured out, you might be struggling in your relationships. If you're struggling in your relationships, you might be excelling at work. On the surface, you might look like you have it all figured out, but you still wake up feeling lost from time to time.

Truthfully, the idea of having it figured out is a concept used to help you feel a false sense of stability. It's a construct in place to avoid feeling embarrassed when that family friend you haven't seen in years asks you how you are. And then you can tell them you checked off all the boxes on the list of what it means to be "successful" according to society's standards.

Let's be real, if you had no one during the holidays asking you about your job or significant other, or when kids were on the way, or when you were going to buy a house, would you care about rushing to get those things done? It is the eyes on us from the outside world that cause us to feel the need to rush our lives. We aren't born with the need to shame ourselves for every little thing, we got that from the story the world taught us: we are only worthy if we "appear" worthy.

The most important thing to understand is the only real testament to success is how we feel inside. This journey back to ourselves and learning who we are at our core, healing from our pasts, and embracing our humanness is the answer to finding this success. It will not come from forcing yourself to be perfect, checking off boxes, or pleasing other people.

Be a good human to others, learn the lessons you are here to learn, and better yourself as you go, and you will be doing *more than enough*.

Unconventional mindset shifts

Slowing down and taking a break from hustling is just as important as working hard.

We live in a world where we are taught that the only way to achieve success is by constantly working without breaks. There are countless books and pieces of advice out there telling entrepreneurs the only way to become rich is to "grind," give up sleep, socializing, relaxing, and everything else good. I would like to challenge this idea. I am not saying you don't need to work hard to achieve success. I am, however, saying that if you neglect your other needs in the process you will pay for it later on. Constant grinding is a recipe for emotional and physical burnout, lack of connection within your relationships, poor health from lack of sleep/exercise/self-care, difficulties with mental health, and high cortisol levels from the stress you are putting on your mind and body. You may create the image you have always dreamed of by hustling day in and day out, but you will suffer the consequences at some point. I've often heard, "Work hard today so you can relax later." The issue I have with this quote is it comes with the guarantee that we have tomorrow. Our tomorrow is never guaranteed.

You can torture yourself now in hopes it will be worth it later, but you don't know if you will have a later. You don't know if you will be able to mend the relationships with those you neglected. You don't know if you will be healthy enough to do all of the things you gave up doing while you were hustling. Creating *balance* and space in your life to take care of yourself is what is going to allow you to create sustainable success. Your connections with others, your physical and mental health, and the emotions you feel day to day will allow you to create a fulfilling life. Yes, you need to do hard things to create the life of your dreams, but *not* at the cost of your well-being.

A person's character and values are the most important things to consider when building a friendship or relationship.

A person's character is who they are at their core. To me, having good character means having integrity. If someone has good character, they are not *just* a good person to your face. A person with good character will show up for you when you aren't around. They will be the same person they are in the outer world as they are behind closed doors. They are genuine and have your best interest at heart. They mention your name in the highest regard in a room full of people.

Hand in hand with character, getting to know a person's values is crucial to understanding who someone is and how they will treat you. Your values shape the way you make decisions, treat other people, and how you show up in the world. If you and your friend, family member, or significant other don't have the same opinion about which diet is the healthiest, you can still have an amazing relationship and have many other opinions you agree on. If you have different values, you will likely want different things out of life, treat people differently, interact in your relationships differently, and have difficulty connecting.

Your values are like a guide of ethics you follow as you go throughout your life. If someone's guide is written differently than yours, they will live by different "rules" so to speak. You can love someone with different values than you, but it will be hard to maintain a deep connection with them. Watch the way people show up in the world. Observe the way they treat everyone: service workers, someone who accidentally bumped into them at the store, flight attendants, or the barista who made their drink wrong. Pay close attention to how they speak about their friends and talk to their family members. Simply observing someone will allow you to learn a lot about their values and character. Listen only to the evidence of what you have learned from watching the way they behave in the world, as words often remain empty without action to show their truth.

You are allowed to decide to do things differently at any point in time no matter how far in you already are.

A common experience people have is they desire to change and do something else but feel like they can't. They feel they are too far into what they are doing, or they have invested too much to change course. With time, you will grow and evolve and so will your desires. It doesn't matter how old you are, *you can* choose at any moment to be different. As long as your decisions are based on your true heart's desires, there is nothing wrong with deciding what you once thought was for you isn't any longer. If something doesn't feel aligned or right to you anymore, you are under no obligation to continue. You are allowed to prioritize your happiness over money invested, time spent, and people who may be temporarily disappointed.

Although it may be scary and a big risk to decide to change, doing what is most aligned and best for you will always be worth it in the end. Maybe you moved across the country and spent a ton of money to ship your car and belongings, but after giving it a fair chance, you decide you hate it. You are allowed to move back even though you already invested so much. Maybe you said yes to an engagement because you thought you wanted to marry this person, but later on you decide you are unhappy. You might feel obligated to get married because of all the time and energy people spent on planning the wedding. You are still allowed to change your mind and do what is right for you. Money returns and disappointment blows over. Maybe you spent years in school to become a doctor but later realized you hate the profession, and it makes you miserable. You probably feel like you can't change your mind because of all the work you put in. *You are once again allowed to change your mind.* You do not have to be miserable in life just because time, money, or feelings were invested. Your mental well-being should always be of the highest importance, and you are allowed to make big changes to prioritize it, even if it feels terrifying.

You aren't lost, it just feels like you are because you are disconnected from your true self.

When you feel lost, you feel like your future is uncertain. You might feel like you don't know what your next steps are, who you are, or what your place is in this world. However, there is a part of you inside that *already* has all of the answers. You don't need to search the world for it like you may think you do. This part of you holds wisdom. It is who you inherently are; who you would be even if everything was taken away from you. You, at your very core. Sometimes we get disconnected from this part of ourselves because of our life experiences. We may go through situations that make us forget what we love, desire, and who we are. Or maybe, we never knew how to learn those things in the first place. Your answer to feeling lost lies in going on this journey of building a relationship with yourself as an adult. Learning who you are, understanding what you desire, and listening to your inner voice will connect you back to your true self. You *feel* lost because you haven't yet built the inner security from creating a relationship with yourself. When you create this security you will still feel grounded, even when you don't know what is coming next. You won't feel lost even if you have no real idea of your future. The difference is simply a shift in how you feel internally and your perspective on where you are in life. It's you deciding to plug yourself back in after being unplugged for a while.

Failure isn't negative, our perception of what we believe failure means causes us to feel this way.

As humans, our lack of action is rooted in the fear that we may fail at what we are trying. There's a part in many of us that believes if we try and fail, we won't be able to handle it. That we are losers in life and will never achieve our dreams. I want to encourage you to change your perspective on failure to this: to fail is to *learn.* Trying something and failing at it teaches you what you need to do better the next time. Failing allows you to gain experience and adjust to improve.

Think about it like this. You might initially say to yourself, "I'm scared to fail." But would you ever say to yourself, "I'm scared to learn?" You wouldn't, but the difference between the two words is the emotion they hold. The word fail holds the emotions of fear, rejection, and despair. The word learn holds the emotion of improvement, progress, and satisfaction. If you allow the fear of what you think failure is to hold you back, you will never do anything new. You will never allow yourself to become who you want to be, nor improve upon what you are trying to accomplish. But should you allow yourself to try new things even with the possibility of failure, you open the door to learning and progressing. This is how you create your dream life and the best version of yourself, by allowing yourself to learn from your mistakes over and over again until you master your craft. Failure is not as negative as you think it might be, your perspective on it is. Your 20s are the time to let yourself try things even if you crash and burn the first few times, it is not the time to let your fear stop you from doing what you wish to.

Finding your purpose

There is A LOT of focus on finding your purpose in your 20s. There are billions of people on this Earth, why would we all be destined to find happiness by living the same path? The same goes for your purpose. Every person on this Earth has a unique purpose, but *it may not be what you think it is*. Many people believe their purpose has to be a huge a-ha moment. For a lot of people, it is, which is where we got this idea in the first place.

But your purpose might look a lot different than you imagined it would. It is important to get used to the idea that you may not wake up one day and say, "I got it! I know my purpose!" You may realize what you were destined to do through the simplicity of everyday life.

For instance, you may have this beautiful gift where you can make anyone laugh. You may not have thought much about it, but maybe your purpose is to be a bright light in people's darkness. The older lady you made laugh in the cafe line may not have had the opportunity to connect with another person in a long time, and you reminded her of the beauty of it.

Or maybe you can make people feel heard. You have a way of listening to people where they feel your presence within each of their words. The way you asked the cashier how their day was, and they replied, "It could be better," and you followed with, "Why's that?" You have the gift of listening in a way that allows them to give you a real response. They knew you cared because you were present with them, even for a moment. Maybe no one asked or listened to them for a long time, and you were the one who showed them the love they needed to get through the day.

As humans, we are intricately designed with a bunch of "gifts" (you could also call them skills). These gifts were given to you for a reason, and they might be for your purpose. Your gifts **do not** have to be your career. You might use the knowledge of your gifts to decide your career path, or you might use your gifts to help you succeed more in the regular job you currently have.

As you are going on this journey of building a relationship with yourself and getting to know yourself at your core and within your soul, you will begin to notice your gifts.

You are a surplus of things at your core, in your soul. You are not just a student, daughter/son, sibling, friend, etc. The qualities and gifts you carry in your soul would still be there if you did nothing ever again. They are you. Get to know who you are in your soul.

The more you align what you do during your day with the things that align with your soul, the more you will thrive. It's the difference between putting a plant in a dark room eight hours a day and then giving it only a few hours of sun in the evening. A little bit of sun may help it stay alive and get by, but it's not growing or thriving.

Naturally, when you align your gifts with what you do all day, you will thrive so much more. You will grow and expand all day instead of just existing.

I want to add that it's okay for your career to NOT be your dream job. Sometimes it is okay to simply get by and pay the bills. There is nothing wrong with that and isn't something to be ashamed of. Sometimes we all need periods of life where we just get by. We don't always need to be doing something extraordinary.

The thing is, though, you are reading this book because you are ready to become who you are meant to be. At some point, there will be a time when you crave more. Your soul is going to crave feeling alive and fulfilled. You're a dreamer and you want more out of life than what we are taught is enough.

One of the ingredients in the recipe for becoming your best self and living your dreams lies in listening to your soul and using your soul-given gifts. Everyone is capable of this. Everyone has gifts. If you think you don't, you are likely a bit disconnected from yourself. You have to **meet yourself again**. I promise you there is a reason you are here on this Earth, a purpose you came here with. Even if it seems so simple when you figure it out—such as making people giggle in line at the store.

Trust the process of becoming who you are meant to be. Get to know yourself a little every day. Learn your gifts and start using them any chance you get. Even if you hate your job there are ways you can use your gifts during your workday. Maybe you make people smile more often, provide your coworker with a listening ear, or use your ability to see things from a fresh and unique perspective to help the company expand. The options are endless for making the most of where you are.

I know a lot of you might be either unemployed or working a job you don't love, but please don't feel discouraged if that is your current situation. Believe it or not, there is beauty where you are. Beauty can always be found in our current situation. Choosing to see the good in the present moment does not mean you are settling for it. You can find a way to enjoy your life right now while simultaneously knowing you are actively trying to make changes.

The part that matters here is to make sure you *recognize* when you are in a situation you don't want to be in forever. When you recognize that, you won't get stuck in a place that isn't how you want it to be for too long. You will start taking the steps to grow and evolve out of where you are.

The most important thing you can decide to do when you are unhappy with yourself is to make the conscious decision to accept yourself and all of your circumstances, as they are now.

I'll give you an example of a time in my life when I focused on what I didn't like about my life instead of all the positive aspects. As I have lived out my dreams of being a traveler, I have been privileged to live in new places for months at a time and have my childhood home to come back to when I wanted to take a break. I never thought it made sense to start a lease somewhere when I was gone for months at a time, so I saved money by living with my parents. Every time I came home from a trip, I dealt with post-travel blues. I felt super depressed for a week or so. I felt triggered in my home environment, reverting to old qualities I didn't love about myself (low energy, overthinking, loss of my spark). Every time I went home, I rejected my current circumstances and wished to be elsewhere.

Eventually, I realized this was no way to be. I had to remind myself how lucky I was to have a home to go back to where I felt safe enough to crumble emotionally. I had to remind myself how lucky I was to still have two parents who loved me and wanted me around and how fun it can be in the summertime in Upstate New York, to frolic around my backyard like I did when I was a kid. There was beauty in going back home. There was beauty in all the times I was triggered by my past while at home because it reminded me I'm not quite done healing. The beauty was always there, I was choosing not to see it at first. I was choosing to throw myself a pity party.

If you are constantly placing focus on all of the parts of your life that you are unhappy with, you're leaving very little room for anything to change. The more you dial in on your unhappiness, the more your mind is reminded to dwell on and feel your unhappiness.

Believe it or not, this concept applies to everyone in every area of life. Consciously accepting and acknowledging you are unhappy with your circumstances allows you to lift the focus from all of the things you are unhappy with. Acknowledging you are unhappy is a hard thing to do and is the reason we as humans often resist the way we feel. We don't want to admit defeat. But how can we feel differently if we don't allow ourselves to recognize we are feeling a certain way we want to change?

You might think life has never been worse or you feel completely lost. This makes it hard to see the good in your situation, I get it. I promise you with everything in me that there is power in finding things within you to be grateful for. And there are always things you can find.

The fact that you are here, alive, and able to read this book is one thing you have and can decide to be grateful for. When you decide (again, another simple decision to change your perspective) to accept and acknowledge your hardship as well as find it within you to look for the good in it, you are already well on your way to creating your dream life.

Gratitude

It's easy to get down on ourselves and hate where we are in life. It's easy to wish the days away because lately, they might be awful. It's easy to wish we were somewhere in the future: in love, experienced in our career, more money, better living conditions, etc.

Your reality *is your choice* to a large degree. If you absolutely cannot change your circumstances for whatever reason, understand it is now your choice to change your perspective. Even if you cannot change your circumstances, you *can* change your perspective on them.

For example, let's say you have a job you hate, but you can't quit for another year due to a contract. In this scenario, you do have choices. You can choose to continue to let the job make you completely miserable every single day until your contract is up. Or you can choose to DECIDE to make the best of it. You can find the good in your coworkers and dial in on it. You can decide to feel lucky to have a job in a world where a lot of people struggle to get one. You can decide to show up to work and show more kindness to others, which in turn makes your day and theirs better. The choice *is* yours: look for the bad in your situation and hate your life for the next year or decide to create positivity within a less-than-desirable situation. You have control over your perspective and your choice.

One of my favorite quotes describes exactly how our brains naturally operate. "Your brain will choose a familiar hell over an unfamiliar heaven." Our brains are wired to choose what is familiar. And for a huge percentage of people, what is familiar to your brain are thoughts you hate thinking and feelings that make you feel terrible. Whatever keeps repeating in your life and your brain is what your brain feels familiar with. We will dive deeper into this later.

The point is, it's often *easier* to wallow in self-pity. It would be easier to continue to walk into work every day and focus on how annoying your boss is and how much you hate the tasks you have. But you can decide to take the more challenging route, which will provide you with more benefits than the easier route ever could.

Our future isn't promised to us. We think it is, but we never know for sure. All we have is right now. This is why it is so important to find the good in where we are right now.

Practicing daily gratitude is one of the smallest, yet most powerful habits I have integrated into my life. One of the most essential lessons I learned about gratitude is not waiting to start being grateful. If you wait, it might be too late.

For example, you don't want to begin feeling grateful for your health once you're thinking about it in the past tense. If only after you fall ill, do you realize how grateful you are for your healthy, strong body, then you don't understand how lucky you were to have your health. There are so many things about the human experience we take for granted.

Our health, our strength, our loved ones, our possessions, the food we can afford to eat, the clean water we have to drink, the shoes and clothes we wear, or the hair on our heads. There is an endless list of things we have that we need to recognize the beauty of and hold gratitude in our hearts for.

A habit I try to remember to keep up with is that any time I find myself wanting to complain, I turn it into a statement of gratitude. If I don't want to get up to go to the gym, I remind myself how lucky I am to have a body that can get up to work out. If I complain about being busy with work, I remind myself how lucky I am to have work in the first place. If I complain about having to walk a long distance, I remind myself how lucky I am to have strong legs that can get me where I need to go.

Sometimes it takes a reminder, where you sit down and consider what it would be like if you didn't have all of those things. To realize not everyone is so lucky.

One early fall morning I was aboard a big Greyhound bus headed to New York City, seated in my usual window seat. A woman walked through the aisle looking for her assigned seat on the bus. I observed her as she lugged all of her bags by herself peeking up at the numbers from seat to seat until she found hers. She had oxygen tubes strung through her nostrils and one of the many bags she carried was a reusable grocery bag holding her oxygen tank. She ended up sitting right behind me, and the entire bus ride I could hear the sounds of her breathing in and out and the clicking of the oxygen tank.

At that moment, I was reminded how lucky I was to have strong lungs that could breathe all on their own. I was able to travel from place to place with no concern

70

about whether or not my lungs could do it. I was able to walk freely without having to carry a big oxygen tank around with me. What a blessing!

I spent the entirety of that bus ride thinking about all of the things I was grateful for. The key here was I genuinely felt in my heart how truly grateful I was. I didn't state my gratitude out of politeness or feeling like I had to as a chore.

Weirdly enough, I had written the story above this during the beginning of my trip to Hawaii. But I experienced yet another moment where I felt truly humbled on the *last* day of my trip. I happened to, again, be boarding another bus to get across the island to the airport for my Redeye flight. There was a girl who looked to be in her early 20s speaking with the security guard about how she was trying to get home to a town two and a half hours away, and I heard the guard tell her she wasn't going to be allowed on the bus without shoes.

This sweet, young girl didn't have a *single* pair of shoes to wear. I could tell she was defeated and upset. To this day I don't know her situation, but I do know I immediately felt my privilege in that moment. I remembered I had zipped my flip-flops into the top of my suitcase, so I ran to the guard to let her know I had shoes the girl could have. To me, they were a pair of flip-flops that I would be perfectly okay without. To her, they were the difference between her being stuck somewhere and her getting home safely. I thought about her the whole bus ride to the airport, and it truly reminded me how most people in the world do not realize how lucky they are. Some people do not even have a pair of shoes. The fact that so many of us have multiple pairs of shoes for all different occasions is something taken for granted.

Gratitude is a *feeling* not just a statement. Let me reiterate that. A feeling in your heart and the more you feel it, the more you reap the benefits. When I slip up on my habit of remembering to be grateful, I notice the difference. I am significantly happier when I am grateful. Every. Single. Day.

Michelle Lynn Johnson

Living with courage and self-honesty

One of the bravest things you can do in this life is to have the courage to be honest with yourself. You might not realize it, but we humans lie to ourselves all the time. We lie to ourselves about what we want in life because we think if we dream too big, the pain of not achieving it will be too much. We lie to ourselves about our mental health because if we acknowledge it, it will be time to face those heavy emotions lurking under the surface.

We lie to ourselves about how we have treated people. We make excuses for our behavior every chance we get because if we are honest with ourselves, we will have to be vulnerable by apologizing and admitting our wrongs.

We lie to ourselves about the reasons we choose to avoid going after our dreams every time we make an excuse that rationalizes our fear of doing it. We lie to ourselves about the difficult experience we went through by invalidating the pain of the experience so we can protect ourselves from facing it.

We lie to ourselves about the people who treat us in a way we don't deserve, because if we allow ourselves to acknowledge the truth of that person, we will have to face the pain of confronting them and letting them go for good.

Honesty requires vulnerability and it requires feeling heavy emotions. Honesty requires us to be uncomfortable. In our society, we are fed distractions from a silver platter. We are given easy access to numbing agents: social media, TV, alcohol/drugs, and keeping overly busy in the name of hustling.

Toughness and resiliency do not come from swallowing our pain, they come from feeling it. I used to be a pain distractor, so I know this from experience. This runs deep within my family's roots, to avoid feeling. To avoid vulnerability. At the fault of no one as it has been passed down within generations, never questioned or noticed. But I realized during my journey, I was never going to become who I wanted to be if I avoided vulnerability and my pain.

As I have mentioned a few times in this book so far, I never used to cry when I was sad. I'd just go to sleep or let my phone distract me from it. It was easier to run from confrontation, too. I never wanted to upset people by sharing how I felt. When I first started learning how to share my feelings out loud with others, I would cry every time. I felt embarrassed and vulnerable. I still tend to get emotional when I open up, but I know how important it is, so I'm comfortable with it now. I learned that real strength is developed through teaching myself how to feel deeply and be vulnerable. Not through avoidance.

There will be many moments throughout your life where you wish other people would take the lead. You might wish someone would offer you a series of apologetic words that you know would make a huge difference in your healing. The fact is most people aren't aware of the importance of vulnerability. They aren't aware that difficult conversations can provide deep healing and an even deeper connection.

So, although you may wish you weren't the one spearheading all of the conversations, understanding your ability to create space for those you love to be vulnerable with you is teaching them the power of emotional rawness. This is opening doors for not only your generation to begin to heal, but generations to come. Your willingness to spearhead healing conversations will change the lives of everyone to come. This is the power that comes from having the courage to talk about difficult things.

You may think you have made the wrong decision to open up and be vulnerable if you are met with backlash, but I assure you, your courage was *not for nothing*. When people are not used to vulnerability, they will often retaliate to "feel safe" (subconsciously, I'll explain). Vulnerability **does not feel safe** to someone who doesn't understand it yet because it requires painful emotions to arise and demands to be felt. Showing emotions does not feel safe to someone who has always been taught to only show emotion behind closed doors. If you are met with this backlash, do not worry. The brain is wired to keep us safe from what it deems a disruption to what is familiar. A negative reaction to your efforts is likely a natural response to their brain seeing your words as a threat to their baseline emotional state.

Whether it happens in your lifetime or not, you are planting a seed within your family's generations to become comfortable with vulnerability. That is an insanely beautiful gift. No, not everyone will be ready to experience this kind of vulnerability in this lifetime, but your ability to start the conversation is not in vain.

On the other side of things, your personal healing journey will require you to have this same ability to be vulnerable with yourself. You will feel your *own* brain's backlash in the form of making excuses for yourself and validating the part of you that doesn't want to acknowledge the pain this vulnerability brings up (this is called self-sabotage).

It takes deep courage to allow yourself to see your flaws; and to be able to look at situations wanting to do the *right* thing, instead of wanting to *be* right.

There is nothing easy about confronting yourself when you are in the wrong. There is nothing easy about openly admitting you are sorry for your actions and that you will actively try to be better next time. It would be much easier to lie to yourself and others by gaslighting both of you into thinking you weren't in the wrong. However, sometimes we *are* wrong.

Just because we didn't mean to hurt someone doesn't mean we don't need to take responsibility for doing so. I'd like to remind you of our innate humanness, which means we are subject to making mistakes. Therefore, yes, you will hurt people on your journey of being human.

Everyone has flaws. Everyone has triggers that cause them to act out of character. Our ability to be both aware of these aspects and take responsibility for the actions that come with them is what matters. It's not about changing yourself into a flawless individual, it's about turning yourself into a person who is willing to acknowledge your flaws and stop them from leaking onto other people.

The best way to heal is to feel. Feel the uncomfortable emotions that arise when you have to recognize the qualities in yourself you aren't proud of, when you have to be vulnerable and open up about things you aren't used to talking about, and from someone watching you cry when you bring up a difficult topic.

Holding resentment, anger, shame, and guilt will kill you slowly. Maybe not literally, but it will slowly kill your bright light. It will eat you alive and spill onto everyone in your path. It will kill your dreams. You might not realize it consciously, but you might be scared to let go of that resentment or anger you have for someone else, or even yourself because you might be scared that if you let it go, it means you have to forget it. You don't have to forget it. Your willingness to let go of anger, resentment, shame, and guilt just means you care enough about yourself and your future to stop letting it consume you and alter your life.

You will always remember what that person did to you to cause you to resent them. You will always remember what stupid decision you made that makes you feel ashamed. You will always remember this pain in some way. Feeling it does not diminish or invalidate your experience. Feeling it allows you to take back your future, not erase your past.

When you hold onto these emotions, you give them power over you. Take your power back by acknowledging them and allowing them to be felt and processed.

These emotions are demanding to be felt, and that is why they are sitting in your heart and your body. They aren't going to go away. They will either show themselves without your awareness in your relationships and everyday life, or they can be felt and processed within your awareness in the safety of the environment of your choosing. I applaud your bravery and courage to decide to be honest with yourself.

As I mentioned previously, there is always an easier option to take. This includes our relationship with both ourselves and others. There is always the choice to choose to ignore the truth of situations to spare yourself from feeling the heavy emotions that may come up.

This option has the same consequence as any decision that results in you deciding to stay in your comfort zone: you stay the same. This is the exact reason why most people stay the same their entire lives. This is why people settle for surface-level relationships, opt for numbing agents to cover up what they really feel and think inside, and never live a life they love.

To grow and to live the life you have always dreamed of requires you to choose the more difficult option in most situations while you are beginning your journey of growth.

As we will talk about extensively in the mindset portion of this book, anything we do over and over will eventually become familiar to our brains. This is what it means to create a habit. You must create the habit of choosing to get uncomfortable in the name of healing. The more you do this, the *less* uncomfortable it will be and the *more* you will be rewarded. Vulnerability and self-honesty = two more of the key ingredients to your inner healing and evolution into who you were meant to be.

Developing your intuition and self-trust

Your intuition, otherwise known as your heart, your gut, or your inner knowing, is one of the most important tools you have within you. We all have it. We can all tune into this powerful tool we are born with.

The more connected you are to yourself and the more aligned you are with your soul, the stronger your intuition will be. Think about it. If you are constantly second-guessing every decision you make, you aren't going to trust your inner voice or the feelings in your body.

If you are living out of alignment with your soul and living a life you hate, you are going to be disconnected from yourself and your inner power. The best part is that no matter how disconnected you get, you can always reconnect with this part of you. It is always within you and will never leave.

Many people have mentioned to me that they have a hard time hearing their intuition because of anxiety. Anxiety does cause you to second guess yourself and overthink. Anxiety can't take that inner knowing away, although it might cloud your ability to hear it if you aren't used to listening.

You *do* know what your intuition feels like because you *have* experienced it before. At some point, you have experienced the ease that comes with knowing something is right for you. What is right for you does not panic you or spark your body into fight or flight. It feels safe. Your intuition is a *calm knowing*. I like to think of it as a peaceful ping of guidance.

The way I see it, intuition can be situational. Of course, there are intuitive feelings that could save your butt in potentially dangerous situations, such as people describing a time they waited at a green light for another second because they heard or felt a feeling to wait, and seconds later a huge truck ran the red light. If they ignored their intuition the truck would have crashed into them. Or there are stories where people met this incredibly charming individual but had this deep feeling telling them to get away from that person, and it ended up that the person was a known serial killer.

77

I think people feel this is the way intuition works all of the time. Most of the time, however, it won't be like that for the majority of people. Intuition doesn't always have to be about big life decisions. Your intuition is available to you at all times should you choose to listen.

The perfect example is how I use my intuition as a traveler to meet people. When traveling as a solo female traveler, I don't have a lot of room to make bad choices about who I am around and what I do. This could cost me my life if I do the wrong thing thousands of miles away in a new country.

I have learned, ESPECIALLY with people, that your intuition is critical when developing connections with others. Your intuition can sense things you otherwise wouldn't be able to pick up on. Sensing a person's energy can tell you whether this person is trustworthy or if they have pure intentions. This sounds crazy, to not use logic when judging someone. But logic can't instantly pick up on things like energy can. Logic will tell you to take time to get to know someone before deeming them safe. Like I said, I don't have that luxury of time when I am traveling.

I have met countless people who I didn't feel safe around straight away and they did nothing wrong. They said all the right things and acted in a normal way. As it turned out, those people ended up being shady. They were people who had the characteristics of what I like to call "emotionally unsafe" people. I don't mean they are necessarily dangerous serial killers, but they are the type of people to lie, belittle, manipulate, and use you for their benefit.

Using my intuition during my trips has helped me determine a person's intentions, choose the right friends, choose the right work trades with the best hosts, and stay away from people who didn't have my best interest in mind. People ask me how I always make friends while traveling and I owe it to my intuition and my ability to know who I can trust because of it. I know which people are safe to pour into and develop a connection with.

For me, after paying close attention to myself for the past few years, I have *learned* how to hear my intuition. And no, my intuition is never in the form of hearing words. I don't hear a voice in my head that says, "No, don't do that!" or, "Yes, this is right."

The way you hear your intuition is going to be unique to you. I can't tell you what it's going to feel like because you might get intuitive feelings physically or in visions, sounds, etc. No one can tell you except you. You might have absolutely no idea what your intuition feels like yet, and that's okay. It's all part of the process of building a relationship with yourself. I will tell you though, that however you do sense it, it will feel safe when something is right for you.

Had you asked me during college or before that, I would have had no clue what my intuition felt like. I was too disconnected from that part of myself and filled with anxious thoughts to listen closely enough to hear my intuition. That, or I honestly didn't care enough to listen because I only wanted to have fun, and it wasn't important enough to me yet.

I have learned that when things are right for me I feel safe and calm, and I don't feel the need to overthink the course of action. I know what feels right to me because I listen to how my body feels when I think about it. I look for that safe feeling. When things are wrong for me, I don't feel good at all. My nervous system is dysregulated, I overthink, my heart races, or I feel weary. There is no calmness whatsoever when it comes to things that aren't right for me.

As someone who struggled with anxiety for a long time, it was hard to recognize this was a sign things weren't aligned for me. I often felt physically anxious for no apparent reason. But I truly learned what it felt like when things **were** right for me. I learned how when I listened to that safe and calm feeling, I was always led down a path of alignment with my soul.

Any time I ignored that anxious feeling my body felt when something was wrong for me, I would learn my lesson later. To explain, I'll use an example of a relationship I formed in college before I was familiar with all of this (as well as familiar with myself). I have a distinct memory of feeling very anxious after I met this person and having a series of chaotic, spiraling thoughts about whether or not I was ready for a relationship. I remember something felt off and I found myself asking friends about how I should feel. Part of me always knew something wasn't right since I couldn't stop questioning how I felt in the beginning. I also distinctly remember the moment I declared to myself that I was going to ignore these feelings. I said to myself, "No, you just have no experience in a relationship so it's just the newness of it. You'll get over it."

After some time went on and the relationship ended, it became very clear to me those feelings in the beginning were my intuition telling me, "Nope, not right for you." I knew it from the start, I was *not* ready for a relationship at all during that time in my life. I had a ton of healing and soul-searching to do. Ignoring this intuitive feeling led me to hurt not only my feelings but another person's as well. Being young, that happens. That's part of learning, growing, and experiencing life. That experience was meant to happen so I could learn from my mistakes, like everything else we go through in life. In this case, one of the lessons I have taken with me to this day is what my intuition sounded like when things were wrong for me.

Things that are not right for you will feel like you are forcing a puzzle piece into the wrong part of the puzzle. You can push it into place and try to convince yourself it's the right piece, but after some time you see the colors don't match around it and the size isn't exact. It works in the beginning, but when you go to match another piece to keep building the puzzle, everything starts getting out of place. It's like a ripple effect after that, every piece is the wrong color from then on and the picture you are trying to complete doesn't make sense anymore. You knew when you first put down the piece it wasn't quite right, but sometimes it takes us more time to realize what our intuition knew all along. The same goes for life decisions. We might have an intuitive nudge in the beginning that it's not right for us, but when we are still learning what that feels like, it can be hard to listen. But after we ignore that feeling, just like the puzzle, things continue to feel off. Our life starts going in a direction that doesn't feel authentic to us.

Intuitively making decisions is going to come with learning to trust your inner feelings. As I said, your intuitive feelings will emerge in their distinctive way. No other person can determine this for you because when someone else looks into your situation, they use logic and outside information to help you. Your intuition is not necessarily rooted in logical facts, it's an inner knowing of what is aligned for you.

Consider this: you get a job offer in a new city. On paper, everything seems great. Great location, salary, and your ideal role. However, you have this deep sense something isn't right about the situation. Something about it doesn't offer your nervous system a feeling of peace and calmness, and you can't seem to shake this feeling.

This is an intuitive warning because your subconscious mind can sense something about the situation your conscious mind can't necessarily pick up on. On top of this, if you ask someone else for their perspective, they are only going to see the outside facts: it seems like an amazing opportunity, great salary, perfect role for you. An outside person won't have the same internal feeling you do.

An important thing to note is that if you have continuously experienced something bad with relationships, for example, your brain will try to feed you all sorts of negative thoughts that align with the story from your past. You will have to work on letting all of the initial *thoughts* that come up when meeting someone new or taking a new job opportunity pass without giving them much focus. Your thoughts aren't what you should refer to while you're still working on healing your stories around things that haven't worked out for you in the past. It's the feeling within your body you will get in touch with and listen to.

You won't need to consult any outside sources or look for any logic to make your decision because you'll just know. You will trust yourself. Consider the past to get clues on how your intuition comes through for you. This might feel confusing for you at first if you are an anxious person as I was. Naturally, you are going to start to question if everything is your intuition speaking. This will take practice, be patient with yourself. By building your self-trust in other areas of your life and working on your mindset, you will naturally start to know which feelings to trust. This is all part of the process when learning yourself.

Michelle Lynn Johnson

Grieving a past self

Grieving a past version of ourselves; what a complex concept. To think you can grieve for a period in your life—a version of you that once was and is no longer. No one talks about this. Grief is seen as something you only experience for someone who has passed away. But the thing is, grief means "deep sorrow."

Believe it or not, it's a common feeling associated with life transitions. Think about it. You have heard stories of someone's forty-five-year-old dad randomly buying a sports car and divorcing his wife for seemingly no reason. Everyone calls that a mid-life crisis. "Oh, no worries, Jim is just having a mid-life crisis, it happens."

Well, what is a mid-life crisis? Essentially, it's the reaction that comes from someone experiencing grief for a past version of themselves. Since most people don't discuss grieving a past self, or that heavy emotions will arise from leaving that self behind are to be expected, people freak out. As I've explained before, without having the tools to properly recognize and feel heavy emotions people often have extreme reactions to them.

Transitioning into new stages of life can be quite a painful experience for people to deal with. We may long for the comfort that came with our younger self, for the freedom we used to have, for a time in our life when things weren't so stressful, and feeling like life won't be as good as it was during a certain time in the past.

People in their 20s go through this same crisis, let's call it a "quarter-life crisis" (I've heard this term thrown around a few times and I think it's fitting).

The list of reasons is a mile long: pressures to have it all together, the fear older adults instill that life will never be as good as it was in their youth, confusion about a career path, confusion about where to live, confusion about relationships, you name it.

More people are pushing a "plan" onto 20-somethings than people supporting them in their unknown. Many people are in the ears of 20-somethings saying things like, "When are you moving out of your parent's house?" "When are you going to go to grad school?" "You can't complain, life is much harder once you're older," or, "When are you giving us grandkids?"

I will be the one who reminds you that you are allowed to take time to grieve your old self. You are allowed to be sad you won't be who you were as a kid. You are allowed to be sad that life took it up a notch on the responsibilities meter.

Allow yourself to feel these heavy emotions without shame. There is nothing wrong with feeling them during this time of your life. You are like everyone else in that way. You aren't alone in feeling lost and nostalgic for the past: almost EVERYONE feels this way at some point.

Don't bully yourself when you need to have your own back. Imagine your future child coming to you for advice when they reach their 20s and feel all these heavy emotions.

You'd support and love them, even if you didn't have all the answers. You would take them into your arms and remind them they are doing enough and will soon get through it. You would shower them with compassion and kind words.

You would not shame, bully, or pressure them to make decisions and know it all. You'd see how young they truly are and how they have time to figure it all out. You wouldn't think of them as a failure.

You would see how much they were like you when you were their age, and you'd see the world is their oyster during this time of their life.

Treat yourself this same way and grant yourself the same grace. There is no world where your solution to someone going through a hard time would be to belittle them.

It isn't a coincidence that many graduates deal with what is called "postgrad depression." I think a lot of people wonder why this happens to graduates. This happens because they are grieving who they were in their youth, specifically their college self. They are losing their community and sense of purpose, and their new purpose may not be secured yet.

Humans are happiest when they sense they are moving forward in life. If someone feels like there is no clear answer on where they are going next, or they feel like they are stuck in the same place, depression often arises. This is postgrad life for many.

Although this sounds rather dark, there is a bright side to all of this. With this knowledge, you can understand that this will pass. When you can dive right in and start creating your life in the ways you do have control over, you can regain your sense of purpose.

As for getting over the grief of losing your past self, this too will lessen. You will probably always cherish this part of you and may feel nostalgic for this part of you from time to time, but it won't always feel so heavy. You will learn to fall in love with the next version of you, an even better version. A more evolved and wiser version you will create. In time, you will accept that you can't go back to your college self or your youth, and it will be easier to do so as time passes.

The best part of this next season of your life is that *if you choose* to do so, you get to craft your life to be as you want it. In your youth, you are told what to do and who to be. Now, you get to be the one calling the shots. You will know to decide to embody the qualities you desire in this next-level version. You will get to live a life you are so excited by because YOU chose and created it.

You will create a bond with yourself that is stronger than it ever has been. You will know yourself better than ever and will make decisions with ease because of it. You will struggle less with life's difficulties because you will learn perspectives and tools that create resiliency.

Everyone says childhood is when you are the freest, but I'd argue you are freer now. You have no one telling you what to do next or what to do with your day as a young adult in your 20s. No one is holding your hand telling you how to do life anymore. Your slate is completely clean for you to make it as you want it to be. Children have beautiful perspectives on life because life is mostly just fun for them. Children hold innocence that allows them to dream as big as they want, and no one tells them they are wrong for it.

Those childlike eyes you once saw the world through are still within you, and you can choose to look through them again. You can choose to believe the world is your oyster and life is fun every day. You can create excitement in the little things. You can use your imagination again. You can decide to be who you were before the world told you who you should be.

So although you may be experiencing the weight of the world on your shoulders and the grief of who you were, you are about to enter a time in your life where it feels a little better each day. By deciding to read this book I know you are actively doing the work to get out of the hard part and into the thrilling part of your 20s.

This isn't to say your 20s will be perfect, but I am certain that if you implement what you learn in this book you will get through the mess more easily and you will be on the way to living a life you love.

Soul knowledge

As I have gone along on my journey of life, I discovered what I would call "soul knowledge." I would describe this as knowledge that comes from within our souls, no one taught it to us.

Have you ever known something but don't know how you knew it—not that you forgot where you learned it, but you are certain this knowledge just popped up in your mind and you somehow knew it? That is soul knowledge.

For me, I stopped studying religion in the way of reading the bible or going to church and having someone else teach me about it. I don't believe in judging the way someone finds God, the universe, faith, love, or meaning in life. I don't feel that one religion needs to be the truth for everyone on Earth and that some religions are wrong. To me, who are any of us to say that? None of us are God, so why do we get to decide that other humans who worship other religions are wrong simply because they are different from us?

However, being someone very open to learning about all religions throughout my traveling experiences, I have come to notice a lot of what I am learning in my life is exactly aligned with a message in the Bible or a quote from a Buddhist monk. Suddenly it makes complete sense. It's like my soul knew this knowledge naturally and by existing and learning through life, I pulled it out.

This is why I believe we can only learn certain lessons and concepts in life when our soul is ready to. You may have heard the same quote 100 times throughout your life, but it never made sense to you. You may have heard the same bible verse explained 50 times, but it never hit home. Until the day it *did*. Until the day you realized how much that quote, bible verse, or piece of advice aligned with your current situation, and you finally understood the meaning on a deep level.

You may have told your friend to break up with her boyfriend 50 times throughout their four-year relationship because you could see how horrible he was for her. The fact is, your saying that was never going to make her break up with him. Not until she was *ready* for the advice you were giving, was she going to be able to truly hear you. So it might take her four years to take off the rose-colored glasses and see the truth about him.

Your mom may have been warning you your entire life about one-sided friendships, but you weren't ready to let go of some of your friends. Until you learned for yourself and were ready to accept it, you didn't hear her. Her words didn't resonate *until they finally did*.

You might want all the people you love in your life to be as excited as you are about all of the exciting new self-help information you are learning. You want them to do well, so you share it with them. You may recommend a book or a movie, but they never read or watch it. Of course, you're disappointed, because you want them to experience a better life like you are. But this lesson applies to them, too. They might not be ready to go on the journey you were ready for. The words in this book or the next one won't resonate for them *until one day it does*.

We spend a lot of time in our lives trying to help people who aren't ready. We may spew unsolicited advice because we love people, and we don't want them to struggle. We want to put them on to better things. We want them to find true love. We want them to live their dream life.

This isn't to say you can never share a suggestion unless you are asked, that you can never give advice, or that you can never put people on to the knowledge that changed your life. You can. Every time you do so, you are planting a seed in some sense. Those seeds may need to be watered and put in the sunlight for a while before they begin to sprout.

The message here is that we cannot force people to be ready to change. We cannot force people to take our advice. Advice should be given out of love, and we cannot allow ourselves to become angry with those who don't take it. They might not be ready for your advice, or it might not be the right advice for their ears at that moment.

People have their soul knowledge they are meant to uncover in their lifetime. Some people aren't meant to grow and evolve as much as the next person is, and that's why you probably know some people who have been the same their entire life. We must accept the uniqueness of our journey and the journeys of those we love.

I'm sure there are a lot of therapists out there who have seen some clients grow immensely in one month and others who hardly grew at all over the years. Everyone's path is different.

Allow your soul to discover what it naturally knows and is meant to know in your lifetime. Your openness to learning, growing, and listening to your heart will unlock all of this for you.

Your ability to learn and listen to your soul is a choice you have to make. You must believe you have all of the love, answers, and capability inside of you already–because you DO. You were never lost, everything was always within you, you just became disconnected from the part of you that could hear it.

Sometimes I think about how MUCH I have learned in the past five years of my life. I truly have learned more than I could have ever imagined. I have grown more and evolved into a person I didn't think I would be for many more years. I am proud of that, but I know it came from my choice to be open.

All my growth came from my willingness to look within myself. It came from me looking into my past and allowing me to be honest with myself about the things I've gone through and the events that have shaped my beliefs and mindset. It came from me holding myself accountable when I was not being the person I wanted to be. It came from me getting in touch with the unconditional love inside of my heart that we are born with to better love myself and others every day. It came from me having compassion for myself and others. It came from me choosing to change my perspective to see the good in situations even when it would be easier to sit in self-pity. I chose to believe I knew what was best for me because I did. We all do. No one else knows what is deep in your soul. No one else can feel the pain of your past and do the healing for you.

The incredible part is that no one else has your exact soul knowledge. No one else will come here with the intricately unique soul knowledge you will have in your lifetime.

Your confidence to embrace the uniqueness of your soul will be what puts your natural gifts to good use.

This is how I feel about writing this book. There are a lot of books out there already. But I have always known since I had the idea to write this book that there would be nothing else like it. Why? Because everything I have written has come from within ME. My connection to myself, my soul knowledge, and my heart has written this book. Sometimes I write for a while and after I re-read it, I don't even understand how the words flowed out of me in the way they did. But then I realize, I am open to the part of me that is wise—my soul. And there is no need to worry about whether people will like it, because I know the right people will read it. I know the right people are going to be ready to hear what I am sharing, and my advice will resonate with them. There will be people who aren't ready. But that isn't a reason not to share my message. If I let that fear get to me, the people who need to hear all of this won't be able to.

The same is true for your gifts. The right people will need to hear things said in your voice and with your craft. Someone might have heard the same thing from 50 other people, but when you said it, it resonated. Your uniqueness is connected with their uniqueness. A good mentor once said to me, as her mentor once said to her, "You are depriving the people who need you right now by being scared to put yourself out there."

And it's so true, that resonated with me when she said it. Putting myself out there wasn't about me, it was about all the people who needed my help. I needed to put my fear aside so I could help all the people I was meant to impact.

Imposter syndrome

As someone in my 20s, I have dealt with imposter syndrome like many other people have. The classic doubts of, "Who am I to do all of this?" "What makes me qualified?"

Imposter syndrome keeps many people from doing what they want. I sat on my ideas for years before I did anything with them, and I have to say, they were amazing, I just wouldn't let myself put them out into the world.

I let everything fester within my mind until I thought it was perfect enough to do something with. I wasted a lot of time waiting to be ready and to feel like I was good enough to do what I wanted to do.

How was I ever going to do anything if I waited for perfection? If everything stayed in my mind, it would never be out in the world to be crafted and evolved with time and experience.

I was *scared* people would criticize me and tell me I was not qualified enough to do what I was doing. I, mostly subconsciously since it took me a while to realize it, believed other people telling me I'm not good enough at what I do would mean it was true.

So I sat in the waiting room of my mind waiting for someone to call my name to let me know it was my turn to be good enough to put my ideas out there.

Spoiler alert, no one was coming to save me from my own limiting beliefs. But then I realized, I am allowed to believe I am good enough without the validation of anyone else. I am allowed to be born with the gift of helping others and use it how I choose to, especially if I am using my gift for the good of all. There aren't any rules to my life, but before this realization, I was creating rules and limits. I was creating rules based on what my old limiting beliefs were telling me was true about myself.

91

"You're not perfect, you don't get to give people advice." "You're still in your 20s, why should you get to guide other people in their 20s?" "People are going to hate your work because it goes against what a lot of people believe—you should play it safe instead."

Those were just some of the negative, self-limiting thoughts I was allowing to keep me stuck. There was no truth to the thoughts I was having, but yet I was letting them control me. I know now I am more than capable of sharing my wisdom because I AM wise. I HAVE helped many, many people with my words and my ability to hold space for them. Age does not equate to the level of wiseness you have. Qualification and a piece of paper do not *always* mean better.

I wanted to share this because I know a lot of you may feel the same way if you have a skill you are naturally good at but didn't get a degree in it and have the piece of paper giving you the go-ahead to feel worthy. It would be quite a shame if you didn't share with the world the things you are good at because you didn't learn them in school. Real-life experience is often just as good, if not better. There isn't a right way to do it, because like I have said 1,000 times, everyone is unique. School is the answer for some, but not for all.

For some of you, even IF you have a degree, like the one you probably just graduated with, you might still have imposter syndrome in your new job postgrad. You might feel like, "Did I even learn anything in school? Is it okay for me to be here making decisions with the older adults?" "I don't know what I am doing at all. I shouldn't have been the one to get this job."

Here is the truth. Most people don't know what they're doing at first, even if it seems like they do. As kids, we think adults know it all. We think people in suits and business attire have it all together. We think because they do, we should too. I promise you; most people are winging it or have done so at some point in their lives. You will figure it out the more you experience everything. You will learn as you go. It's okay to feel the way you do, you're **not** the only one. Ask questions, be teachable, and be open. You will grow in your career the same way you will grow in your personal life.

You weren't put on this Earth to hide your gifts and be too scared to use them. You deserve to let yourself be new at something without torturing yourself into backing down.

Different actions, different results

Before we move on to the next part of the book, I want to make sure all of this hits home for you. I figured a good way to do this was to help you look at your world from a different lens once again.

I want you to consider something for a moment. How many people around you are truly happy in life, truly fulfilled, and went after their wildest dreams?

I think you will come to realize the majority of people settle. The majority of people get stuck within their comfort zone, accept where they are in life, and don't feel like it's possible to change.

Don't let this be you. I am sharing all of this information with you, so you have the tools to thrive in this life, and I hope the advice I share hits home enough to impact your perspectives on living.

As much as it has been forced onto us since we were children that success comes from a well-paying job and having lots of material things, I urge you to create your definition of success.

To get you thinking, here is my definition of success: success comes from living a life where you are undeniably present in each moment, you feel alive and fulfilled with the things you are doing most often, and you spread and feel love as much as you possibly can.

I promise that when you die, although no one truly knows what happens to you afterward, none of the money and material items you acquired will matter. Who you are as a person is what will be remembered. All of the little moments will matter and add up: all of the times you shared a simple smile with a stranger who needed it, the times you had a conversation with someone that forever changed that person's perspective of life, or the moments you silently supported someone by providing them your presence.

This is why it is so important for your character and integrity to remain throughout your journey. Never allow your hustle to change who you are at your core, and continuously remember to check yourself. Integrity first, *always*.

Remember, creating real change in your life starts with opening your mind to new possibilities, perspectives, and ways of thinking. Please *allow* yourself to feel empowered by the new possibilities that lie within changing your mindset, habits, and life. I urge you not to shut yourself down because you currently feel you might not be capable of change or living differently. Fight against the voice from the past that chimes in to remind you that none of this could work for you. This voice is wrong.

I know with certainty every one of you is capable of incredible things unique to your passions and desires. The only thing in your way, for now, is you. You are, however, about to get out of your way and change your life for the better *just* by remaining open to the possibilities of what lies ahead in your future.

There are many pessimists in the world. The people who will constantly remind you of the bad side of things, how things could go wrong, and serve up reminders of why life is hard and sucks on a silver platter. Every piece of advice in this book could have an argument created against it by a pessimist. I am pushing you to remind yourself there is no benefit to being a pessimist besides keeping yourself where you are now. There will be plenty of people who hear advice like this and grumble to themselves, "Well, that only works for some. I don't have a choice. I have to suffer, and I don't have another way around it." And the fact is, that is true for them. *Because they believe it.* So, of course, they will continue to prove to themselves over and over again why life is hard and sucks for them and why all life advice is bullshit. Your brain is designed to do that for you. To find evidence for and prove your beliefs to be true. Do not let anyone encourage you to question your capability and ability to create a happy life if they are not happy themselves. They are the ones who will drag you down with them.

Try something different. I promise you have nothing to lose from trying a different approach to life than you have thus far. You might create a better life than you ever thought was possible for you in the process.

Part 2:

Workbook & Action Steps

My childhood story

I want to show you exactly how I took this knowledge and implemented it into my life so you see how this can change the life of an average person. So let me rewind and take you back to who I was before I started building who I am now. There were a few key experiences during my childhood that impacted the way I operated in the world.

The person I was before I discovered mindset work and began my healing journey is very different from the person I have become in many ways. However, I don't see who I was as a *worse* version of me or a version of me I wished I hadn't been, just a version of me who wasn't quite ready to grow into who I was meant to become. This version of me, who hadn't yet learned everything I was meant to, was like an old house before it was torn apart and rebuilt. The foundation of the house, my morals, values, and soul, were the *same* throughout the building process. As the person I was meant to become was built, I gained more of the things I needed to feel secure and whole again. I tore down old rooms that held memories of resentment, pain, or numbness. I knocked down the pillars that held old beliefs, ones I carried with me since childhood that couldn't hold me up anymore and were holding back the creation of my new home. I rebuilt the walls of the home within me with love, care, and extra attention so they could stand tall and strong throughout the rest of my life, no matter what storm came through to try and knock them down. I decided what I wanted my home's interior to look like, no matter what it looked like before. The creation process was totally mine, regardless of what it looked like in the past. I realized I was free to build the person I *wanted* to be, not the person I thought I was or had to be.

But before then, since I was a very young girl, anxiety was something I identified with. The crazy part was, I never actually *knew* what anxiety was. I just knew what it felt like, and it became a part of me to some degree. I learned what the definition of anxiety was once I went away to college. Still, I was already too familiar with all the symptoms: daily butterflies in my tummy, shaking hands, red face, racing heart, and spiraling worrisome thoughts.

I never talked about it, though. I don't think most people in my life knew I had anxiety, except when I expressed out loud something I was specifically anxious about—usually school presentations or riding competitions, which everyone is nervous about, so it didn't raise any red flags.

Going hand in hand with the anxiety I felt, I was greatly affected by the identity I was given by adults and other kids that I was shy. I didn't feel comfortable being talkative to a lot of people, only the people I knew were my safe people. I was a sensitive and observant child; I noticed every little shift in mood or energy in whichever environment I was in. A superpower now, a recipe for overstimulation and stress back then. I would absorb the moods of those around me and feel my responsibility was to protect them. I would feel extremely anxious when I felt I had no control over people's low moods, on top of the fact that I would take on the emotions they were feeling as my own. I constantly carried the weight of the world on my shoulders because I felt it was my responsibility to hold it for others.

I didn't realize this at the time, but looking back, I took safety in my quietness unless I felt you were someone who I could trust to show myself to. Due to the way people around me reacted, I began to internalize this as a bad quality I held. Kids giggled when my face turned red or I spoke too softly, and my classmates would yell, "We can't hear you." Teachers knocked points off my grades for lack of participation. I'm not saying it was the worst thing ever compared to what many kids go through, but being the quiet kid in school was certainly no easy feat. Quietness is not digestible for most. Most people feel uncomfortable in silence. Therefore, I struggled in school, in fact, I *hated* it. I grew to fear raising my hand and being randomly called on—I feared *all* attention. I was afraid to speak up for myself. I lacked boundaries and tended to let people walk all over me. I was terrified of confrontation so I would rather let people make me uncomfortable than say something. Since all of this was something I experienced throughout my entire childhood and into college, it became a part of who I thought I was destined to be, until I learned otherwise.

Despite being a quiet kid who struggled with anxiety, I was also extremely determined and self-motivated. I always knew before I truly *knew* that I was meant to live a little differently. I hated school because it gave me anxiety, but I recognize now that I also felt trapped in a school schedule. I hated the routine of doing the same thing every day and having no say about it.

There were many moments throughout my childhood where my determination was my greatest strength. I was this little girl with a quiet, soft exterior, but I always had a fire lit within me that helped me achieve what I wanted to. This quality helped me tremendously when I started riding horses at the age of ten. I fell in love with the sport instantly. I knew I fell in love with it because I would cry if I couldn't go to a riding lesson, but when I played soccer, I would cry that I *had* to go to practice. My mom used my riding lessons to get me to go to school, since if I missed school, I had to miss my lesson.

I wanted to be the best rider I could be from day one. I begged my coach to let me canter when I had only taken a few lessons and wasn't balanced enough yet to do more than a slow trot. I was *fearless* in the beginning, something I had never experienced in my daily life. Time stopped when I rode, I could step out of reality for a little bit. This was my favorite thing about riding.

The hard truth of equestrian sport is if you aren't wealthy, you naturally have a huge disadvantage. My parents were middle class when I was growing up, but not even close to the type of wealthy you need to be to thrive in the hunter-jumper world. Still, I was hungry for success in the sport. I was lucky enough to grow up during a time when it was common to be a "barn rat," meaning I spent all of my free time at the barn asking my trainers for saddles to clean and stalls to muck. I learned how to be a good horseman and spent more time on the ground with the horses than I did riding them. I loved the horses more than the sport itself.

The anxious personality I had developed during school and in my personal life started spilling out onto riding, causing it to go from solely fun to being something that sometimes caused me stress. Although my parents always made it work for me the best they could and never made me feel bad about it, it never changed the part of me that felt this immense pressure to have something to show for all of the money they invested in my dream. I felt incredibly guilty for falling in love with such an expensive sport and spent a lot of time feeling stressed about it. Guilt and stress are two things that inevitably raise anxiety levels in the body. Again though, I did not understand any of this as a kid. But looking back, it makes sense why my body was so prone to symptoms of an adrenaline rush.

As time went by, I did what I thought I needed to, to move up in the sport. I rode at a few different barns where each trainer and horse taught me something that helped me grow. My parents and some very kind trainers helped me show on the "A circuit," the big horse shows that people from all over the country attend. I was so blessed to have people in my corner who saw how much I loved the sport and helped me pull this off regardless of my financial status.

Because of this experience, I grew strong enough as a rider to make the Division One equestrian team at the college I committed to. I certainly admit that I was never the best of the best, but I *was* passionate about the sport, and I *was* disciplined. Even though riding was not always easy on me mentally, my determination got me where I was. I was beyond thrilled to ride at a Division One level, something most riders dream of. After making the team, I learned how to ride a completely new type of riding from scratch. I was trained as an English rider (the smaller saddle) before college but came out four years later better at Western (the big saddle you picture when you think of what a cowboy would use). This came from hard work, great coaches, and even better horses.

I truly learned the meaning of commitment and dedication during my time on the Western team. I started with no knowledge, competing at the lowest level, to being very confident and competing at the highest level as a senior. To this day, it's one of my proudest accomplishments.

The fire that was always lit within me since I was a little girl was the very thing that allowed me to accomplish all that I did, even during the times when my mind and body didn't want to cooperate. My passion for all I loved remained, even when I had no clue what was going on emotionally. I do believe this is why I always got by and did what I needed to excel, but there was always a battle going on inside me.

This battle with anxiety infiltrated its way into my college life in ways I didn't quite expect, as I hoped life would be different after going away to school. I would purposely find seats in the back of the class because if I had to participate, fewer people could see me. I dropped a class on the first day because our professor told us that we would have weekly solo presentations and the thought of doing that was an absolute "NO" from me. I used to feel sick to my stomach before riding competitions and wouldn't eat a bite until after I was done competing. I shut down mentally during practice if I was having a tough ride because I would feel anxious about disappointing my coach or messing up the horse I was on. I struggled to sleep at night because my mind couldn't seem to stop overthinking and my heart rate wouldn't slow down.

While all of this was going on, there was still that other side of me that fought the inner battle so I could keep up my success. I *knew* going to class was not avoidable. I *knew* I'd have to figure out how to ride even when I was shutting down emotionally. I *knew* I'd have to push through the days when I was shaking, and my heart was beating out of my chest. I didn't know yet that there was a way to end the battle between the two sides of me and create balance within myself.

I think that is what it's like when you have anxiety, at least for me. The part of your brain that wants to try to keep you safe feeds you anxious thoughts and reminds your body everything is a threat, versus the part of your brain that knows the truth and knows what is *really* you. So yes, there were **two** versions of me existing at once during college: the version of me having the absolute best time of my life and the version struggling to navigate existing in a body stuck in fight or flight mode.

What an odd feeling—I was happier than I ever had been in my life, but simultaneously, I struggled with the *same* feelings and symptoms that had lingered in me since I was a young child. This is why, before I learned about mindset during my postgrad adventure, I thought I would always be this way. I thought I was one of the unlucky people on this Earth who would forever deal with a racing heart and an overthinking mind.

When you look back on things you felt or thought about as a kid or a young adult, a lot of things start to make sense. Like how there was a reason why I dealt with anxiety and shyness my entire life—because I was meant to learn how to overcome it so I could share my story to help others. Or the fact that during high school I missed the maximum number of days you are allowed to be absent because the routine of school was draining to me. There was a part of me deep in my soul that always needed to make the rules for my life. These little details about me were the clues that would foreshadow who I evolved into as an adult.

Even the part of me that may have been deemed a bad trait by adults, such as my relentless perseverance, was a quality I held for a reason. I was not the type of kid to stand down in arguments with my parents, and I did not give up when my parents told me I couldn't get things or do things—sorry Mom and Dad. I wrote a few too many letters and made countless PowerPoints convincing my parents about why I should be able to get a dog, cat, horse, guinea pig, hamster, bird, lizard, mouse, etc. I was a convincing saleswoman, and I did get a dog (he was an abused rescue we just HAD to have), a cat (whom I begged to bring home because she was the "ugly" cat no one wanted), eight hamsters over the years, six guinea pigs and one horse.

This quality has helped me greatly in my adult life. As a kid, I always did what I wanted even when it was difficult or not what the crowd was doing. I could have quit riding when people told me only rich kids could make it in the sport, or commented on my short body when being tall and lanky was ideal, or when the stress of being a Division One athlete as well as a student became too much, which it did more than once. I always kept going.

The reason this determination and willingness to follow my path has been key in my 20s is because I continued to live an unconventional life. If I had lived the way I was told to by society, by the expectations of family, or by what everyone else my age was doing, then my life would look very different. I would have gotten a corporate 9-5 marketing job after graduation. I would have settled for the guy I thought my parents would like even though I wasn't ready for a serious relationship. I would have never followed my dream of being self-employed or traveling the world. I had a glimpse into what my life may have turned out like if I hadn't decided to go on this journey of inner healing and growth, and the thought of it scared me.

Because of this, and what I now know to be the quality of courage, I have followed my dreams. My 20s have been rocky, they haven't been smooth sailing in the slightest. I have messed up, lingered in procrastination for a little too long, shamed myself for not doing enough, hit many rock bottoms, and gotten stuck in my comfort zone more than enough times. However, I wouldn't trade any of it. All of it taught me something I was meant to learn to become the person I am today. All the time I spent procrastinating writing this book was for a reason; I had more life lessons to learn to share with all of you.

Instead of going down a path inauthentic to me to please others, I took the route I wanted to take. I probably scared my parents half to death in the process (like the time I got dropped off in the jungle in Hawaii to live in a treehouse for a month with nothing but faith that it would work out) or the fact that I haven't had a regular day job that provides stability since I was freshly graduated.

I have been *so deeply rewarded* for taking this risk. I have been traveling solo since I was 24 after I took the leap and left my routine life in New York behind. This lit a fire in my soul and unlocked parts of myself I didn't even know existed, in the best way. I met friends on these trips I had instant connections with that I consider my "soul friends." These trips have shown me what I need and want out of life to feel alive, fulfilled, and whole. This is why I feel so passionate about sharing my story with all of you. I want every one of you to have the opportunity to live according to your bliss and figure out what brings it to you.

So now that you know a bit more about who I am and how my journey unfolded, I will share with you everything I learned that allowed me to step into my most authentic self and overcome some of these lifelong challenges. This part of the book is the actionable part: the part that holds the steps you can take to begin to implement these habits and mindset shifts so you too, can step into your best self and begin living your dream life.

Of course, it is not as easy as it sounds, healing old beliefs and shedding old habits is by no means an overnight journey. A person's healing and growth journey is *never* linear, meaning it is never obvious, "Oh, that's healed, I'm done now." Healing past wounds that are deeply embedded within you might take time and feeling the same things over and over again, even when you thought you were over it or past it. The decision to become aware of and begin to work on healing the things that are limiting you and that had a massive impact on your life up until now is what will change your life the most. There is no finish line of human perfection that any of us will cross in our lifetime.

Michelle Lynn Johnson

Finding your "why"

To commit to changing your mindset and reprogramming your past self into your best self, you will need to understand *why* it matters to you to make these changes in the first place. As we discussed earlier in the book, if you don't have a strong enough reason to change, you will likely believe your excuses and go back to your old ways of being. This reason to change is called your "why." So let's start there.

Finding your "why" to change will be what inspires you to continue the change even on your most difficult days and what gives you the willpower to do so. Having a reason to keep pushing through during those difficult periods will get you through it. It will aid you in being resilient.

Your motive to change may be very specific, maybe you already know in the back of your mind what it is. For example, maybe you know if you don't create new habits, you will become ill in the future. Or maybe you know if you continue on your current path, the inspiration for dreams you have held for the entirety of your life will die off.

Your first task is going to be creating your own why. Use the questions provided and answer the questions written out in this workbook, in your phone notes app, or even spoken out in a voice memo. Go deep and think about this. Finding your why will be the key to the first door that opens to your new, evolved self.

What will you lose if you never create these new habits? Think about your life in 20-30 years. What will your life be like if you never change or pursue what you want to?

_____

_____

_____

How will you feel in the moment when you are halfway through your life and realize you never did what you wanted to? You need to visualize yourself in the future making that realization. Sit with that feeling. There is a different type of pain that comes from recognizing you gave up on yourself and never allowed yourself to unlock your full potential. This understanding should help you see that the temporary discomfort you will go through in the beginning, when it feels difficult to keep the new habits and form your new mindset, is worth pushing through.

_____

_____

_____

_____

_____

_____

_____

To go deeper: who will miss out if you never change? Is it your future or current children? Is it that dream partner you have been picturing since you were little? Is it your friendships? Think about who in your life will miss out on meeting the version of you who went for their dreams and made the changes to become their best self.

_____

_____

_____

_____

_____

_____

_____

_____

_____

_____

So maybe your motive is just that—the idea of aging later in life and realizing you never changed or did what you wanted to do. To me, this was motivating enough.

Maybe you have something specific and unique to your life, which is also perfect. No matter what it is, figure out a 'why' that is strong enough to move you forward even on your worst days. Waking up and being motivated is not something to rely on, as you will often be unmotivated to do new things outside of your comfort zone until you establish it as a habit.

Make it a constant to think about your why every time you implement new habits. Write it down in your phone notes app, make it your phone background, write it on a sticky note, and place it on your bathroom mirror, anything you need to do to remember this daily. Eventually, it will pop into your mind every time you find yourself wanting to give up on your journey.

Thinking of all the ways you will miss out is a mindset hack called the "pain-pleasure" principle. This principle suggests that people make choices to avoid or decrease pain or make choices that create or increase pleasure. Therefore, using this principle in an exercise will allow your brain to see that the pain will be greater than the temporary pleasure of avoiding your new habits if you do not change. Currently, you have not changed because whether you are aware of it or not, you believe the pain of changing will be greater than the pleasure.

The science behind changing

Our thoughts can create our reality, but how?

Although it might seem obvious, the majority of us don't fully understand that we have control over how we perceive, interpret, and think about the events that happen in our lives. The perspective and interpretation of events that *we choose* will go on to affect our thoughts. Okay, so why does that matter? They're just thoughts, right?

Yes, to some extent, they're just thoughts. Thoughts that are passing by in your mind that you don't pay much attention to are rather unimportant. But thoughts that are focused on and thought consistently over and over will result in specific emotions being felt. Emotions go on to impact our behaviors. So, like a domino effect, whichever thoughts you place importance and focus on will create an emotion within you, which then affects the behavior you display.

For example, you just completed a school presentation. It didn't go as well as you'd hoped. You have an influx of thoughts about this event such as, "I am the worst public speaker of all time. I am never doing that again. I am so embarrassed." You begin to ruminate on these thoughts and think them over and over. Because of this, you continue to feel mortified. The thoughts that you chose when perceiving the event of your presentation created this emotion of embarrassment that you now associate with presenting.

That emotion will go on to influence your behavior. You now associate presentations with feeling embarrassed, so you will go into the next presentation already feeling those emotions. Your behavior is going to be impacted due to those thoughts and emotions: you will outwardly be less confident, tense, and likely perform the same or worse. Or you might avoid presenting altogether to prevent feeling embarrassed again and miss out on opportunities because of it.

Those original thoughts that influenced your emotions and behaviors were yours to choose from the start, but most of us have no idea we have a choice. No one taught us in grade school that we could consciously choose our thoughts or that our thoughts matter in the first place. Most of the time, our thoughts happen automatically—95% of our thoughts happen out of habit, without our awareness! Therefore, why would we know anything different if our brain is doing all the work for us?

This means, though, that a huge majority of the events we have experienced during our lives, our brain interprets all on its own. It chooses thoughts, emotions, and behaviors based on your unique experiences that taught your brain how to perceive things the way it does.

We do not have to let our brain continue to be a record of the past, unconsciously choosing thoughts that don't feel good and resulting in behaviors that don't align with who we want to be.

You have two choices when interpreting your life events: let your brain decide what it wants to think, even if it's negative, or consciously choose a healthy perspective.

Our choices matter so much, even the little ones. If we make it a habit to throw ourselves a pity party after less-than-desirable situations, our brain will automatically register that when something goes wrong for us, it's time to cue the victim mindset. It will become the norm for us to think negative thoughts, feel worse than we did to begin with, and behave in a way that doesn't serve us when we experience hard things.

We have talked many times throughout this book about things we can do to build our resiliency when life doesn't pan out how we hoped it would. This is another one of those ingredients. *Choose perspectives that allow you to flow out of hardship quickly and choose it every single time until it's a habit.*

Eventually, your brain will automatically choose these healthy perspectives. Your mind won't jump to thinking thoughts that keep you feeling horrible. Your mind will work with you to quickly allow you to move on from situations. This is what it means to be resilient.

These are small choices you can start making that will cause massive upgrades to your life. So the next time something negative happens to you, even if it's a silly and quick incident where your patience is tested, remember this; choose to move on instead of dwell and choose thoughts that reflect who you want to be. It matters.

Can you explain the science behind how our thoughts, feelings, and behaviors end up becoming habits? [6,7]

We learned that our brains automatically interpret events and choose thoughts to think based on what they have memorized from our past experiences. Let's dive a bit deeper into this so you see what happens in our brains for these things to become automatic, unconscious habits.

Changing our habits becomes a lot easier when we understand how our brains operate. Understanding the brain allows us to see the science behind why it can be so hard for us to change, why we self-sabotage, and why habits are hard to keep at first. So, with that being said, I want to share with you a basic level teaching of how our brains work related to our mindset and habits.

The adult brain has been studied to have approximately 100 billion neurons. Neurons are nerve cells, known as "information messengers," that send and receive signals to all parts of the human body. When connections between these neurons occur, pathways in the brain begin to form. A neural pathway is a series of connected neurons that wire in the brain to control thinking processes and different body functions. Each time you act, think, or feel something, a neural pathway lights up and it gives meaning to that specific pattern.

There are well-formed pathways in your brain that occur due to doing the same activity, thinking the same thought, or feeling the same emotion over and over again. We can call these our "habit pathways" for the sake of the explanation because these pathways are the habits we carry out automatically without having to think about them. Everything starts as a new pathway, but if it's not practiced repeatedly, the unused pathway will get deleted. It's like when you start to learn a new language but never practice it. You begin to develop the skill, but after time goes by and you don't continue to practice it, you forget everything you initially learned.

A great way to think of the creation of habit pathways is like walking on top of deep sand. At first, there's not much of a path formed and there are only a few footprints. Walking through it is difficult at first and requires extra effort. As you continue to walk through the sand on the same path over and over, the sand becomes flat and forms a path you can easily walk through. You can walk effortlessly without thinking much about it after you form the smooth path.

This is how habits are formed in our brains. When neurons repeatedly communicate the same thought, feeling, or behavior, they form a strong neural pathway for that habit. When a habit is formed, we no longer need to consciously think about doing it. This helps explain why it is difficult to create new habits. At first, it will be unfamiliar to the brain, just like walking through new, deep sand. But, once you complete the new habit consistently, it becomes a familiar pattern to the brain and will no longer feel like a dread to keep up with.

This is exactly why we need to learn ourselves in depth, so we are aware of all of our most consistent thoughts, behaviors, and emotions. You may currently think of habits only as things like waking up and brushing your teeth, scrolling on social media before bed, or driving to work. However, your habits run so much deeper than your daily behaviors. *Most* of our thoughts occur solely out of habit. Think about it this way, you aren't consciously deciding every single thought you think all day every day. This would drive you crazy. This means that almost all of the thoughts running through your mind are happening automatically. This may seem harmless, but those mindless thoughts you have throughout the day could be affecting your life situation more than you might realize.

Everything you do every single day is remembered and stored in your brain as a memory. Those daily moments where you rose to anger thinking about how much you hate the traffic on the way home from work, where you passed by the mirror and thought self-deprecating thoughts and felt ashamed, where you woke up and the first thing on your mind was how much you hate your job and the dread you feel for the day, or where you lay awake at night thinking about all the things you did wrong during the day and made yourself feel anxious. We have all done these without any realization they are powerful actions contributing to the way our reality is unfolding.

Your body will *remember* when you wake up on a Monday that it's time to feel dread, it will automatically feel angry on the way home from work even if today there isn't any traffic, it will automatically feel ashamed passing by a mirror even if you didn't originally feel that way. If you do something every single day, good or bad, it *will* become a habit your brain has memorized.

Your brain is wired to preserve energy by being able to do as many things on autopilot as possible—that way it has energy to use for more important tasks. This also allows us to not become overwhelmed by having to think about every task we complete.

Doesn't it make more sense now, why all the times you have tried to change it hasn't stuck? If we don't commit fully to creating new pathways in the brain (which we now know requires a lot of repetition), it will not memorize the new habit. Changing **requires** consistency.

The harsh reality is that when we live without awareness of our current habits and allow our brains to operate mainly on autopilot, it means we are products of our past and will continue to be if we don't decide to teach our brains new habits to memorize. The good part is that we have the power to change our circumstances by changing what we experience and focus on.

What processes can we try to rewire our minds and create habits that last?

Studies have proven that our brains can be changed as we actively seek out new experiences and information that reflect the future we want to create. This is called self-directed neuroplasticity. By definition, self-directed neuroplasticity means, "The process of intentionally changing the structure of neural pathways in the brain through personal choices."[2,3,7]

To put it simply, when our brain is wired in a way that adversely affects us, our mental well-being will suffer. When our brain is wired in a way that serves us and the future we want to create, our mental well-being will thrive.

Self-directed neuroplasticity can be used to create new, helpful habits by consciously deciding to focus your attention on what serves you. Like everything else we have learned, it is a choice to do something different than what you have been, and it is a skill to be learned and practiced. However, learning to redirect your focus when you notice these old habits coming up will help to rewire your brain in a way that best serves you. Becoming aware of your limiting beliefs, self-sabotaging behaviors, and negative self-talk, will allow you to know what you need to redirect your attention to. For example, if you know you struggle with a victim mindset when things go wrong, notice when you begin having thoughts or behaviors that reflect that mindset and redirect your focus to the new mindset you are trying to implement. You will have the ability to stop your old habit in its tracks and replace it with your new one.

Here are steps you can take to build a healthy mindset:

Continue building your self-awareness so you can successfully learn what needs a redirection of your attention. Negative self-talk that reflects your old beliefs can be replaced with healthy self-talk that reflects the beliefs of the person you want to become. Practicing affirmations is a great way to shift out of negative thought spirals. If shifting your thoughts isn't enough to push you out of a difficult moment, you can choose movement to help you. Get up and go for a walk, turn on a yoga video, or go do an activity that pushes you into the present moment.

Change what you expose yourself to. Remember—your thoughts, feelings, and behaviors are connected. If you constantly expose yourself to social media content that makes you feel insecure, *you are creating a cause* for a surplus of thoughts, emotions, and behaviors that reflect you feeling insecure. If you are constantly around unmotivated and negative people who make you feel incapable, *you are creating a cause* to carry yourself in a way that reflects that. If you constantly watch media that creates fear within you, *you are creating a cause* for you to feel anxious, think fearful thoughts, and behave in a way that reflects that fear. What you expose yourself to will be the difference between you struggling to change and you feeling empowered to change. Choose to read, listen to podcasts, meditations, shows that inspire you or make you happy, choose to be around people who lift you up, etc.

Work on filling space with mindfulness. Oftentimes, we fill empty time and space with mindless thinking that ends up being thoughts that don't serve us. Then, the classic series of events occur; we had too much time to think negative thoughts and therefore we start feeling anxious or depressed and spiral into pity parties about life sucking. Instead, we can use our self-awareness skills to notice when we are in these spiraling thought spells. For example, if we have too much time to think in the car on the way to work, we can intentionally put ourselves in the present moment by deciding to think about all the ways the day can go well, implement new affirmations that reflect our new belief system we are installing into our brains, or turning on a podcast to spark inspiration for feeling motivated. Instead of letting our minds wander, we can choose presence in as many moments as we can throughout the day. When we are present, we aren't anxious or stressed about the past or the future. We can let go, trust more, and build resilience when we choose to be engaged in the moment. If you choose to be here now, you are choosing to release the option of your brain pushing you into the past or creating worry about the future. There is so much power in that!

Remember to remain open to seeing new, more positive perspectives on difficult experiences. We have talked a whole lot in this book about how important our perspective is and how our perspective impacts us. Reminding yourself to see the positive in situations or actively seeking out the lesson in life's difficulties will contribute to rewiring your brain to better serve you. Not only does this allow you to feel better, but it also challenges your brain to differ from its usual way of seeing things based on your past experiences.

Now that we know how important our unconscious habits such as our thoughts are, how do we create awareness without creating obsession? [4]

We now know that our thoughts create our reality, but is there a way to create awareness of our thoughts without creating an obsession? Yes, there is. To not become obsessed with your every thought is to have a true understanding of how your thoughts *actually* relate to you and when they hold power over you.

You can learn the power of your thoughts, not only so you can make the decision to choose ones that serve you, but so you can understand how *little* they relate to you. Your thoughts are not a direct representation of who you are.

Learning about mindset work is meant to help you understand yourself on a deeper level so you can take control of your future—it is not meant to create an obsession or fear. You can choose to use your thoughts to your advantage, but you can also choose to use what you know to take the load off your back when heavy thoughts come. They can breeze by instead of destroying you and *that is all it has to be*.

There is so much benefit to learning about how powerful your mind is. Learning about this completely changed the course of my life. However, I have seen a lot of people learn about this and feel fearful. They may feel guilt, shame, or confusion about events that have taken place in their lives and feel like it's their fault if their thoughts created their reality. They may obsess over their thoughts and fear any negative thought they have is creating something. I also hear plenty of people preaching, "Just think positive!" which bypasses our human experience and simply doesn't allow for constant positivity.

This is the main problem I have with the concept of teaching about how your thoughts create your reality. This concept should empower you, not cause obsession or fear. But I have met many people who feel this way, so I find it imperative to dive into this part of the conversation.

I wanted to find a way to teach this powerful concept while helping people understand there is nothing to fear. There is no need to go overboard obsessing over every thought you have.

Although you might not like the thoughts that are currently going on within your mind, understand that small actions toward changing them are enough. You do not need to obsess over whether every thought you have is "good" or "bad." You simply need to decide which thoughts you want more of and which thoughts you want to feed and give power to.

For most humans walking this Earth, there will never be a reality where negative thoughts completely stop arising. Humans naturally have a large spectrum of emotions that trigger all different thoughts, good and bad, and this will never stop happening.

The main thing I want you to understand is that thoughts that are given no power cannot have power over your reality. Only what you focus on will expand.

Imagine your mind as a body of clear water. Imagine someone sitting on the edge of the water with a tiny dropper filled with dye. The person puts pinks, purples, blues, greens, reds, and just about every color you could imagine into the body of clear water. In the first second when the color touches the water, you see the color beautifully. Quickly though, the color disappears because there is too much clear water, and the color is almost instantly diluted.

Think of your thoughts as the color being dropped into a huge body of clear water. When you don't focus on the thoughts that come in, they simply disappear. They have no meaning or importance, they come and they go just as quickly. Each thought you have is like a tiny dropper of color. It will have no impact on you at all if you allow that.

However, you always have the choice to let the color grow and expand. The person with the little dropper may decide they want more pink, so they get a bucket full of pink dye and pour it into the clear water. The pink sticks around and it looks so beautiful. Think of the pink dye as your "feel good" thoughts. You can choose to allow these good thoughts to expand and continue to make you feel good. You can keep focusing on them until you feel so good from those thoughts that your whole body feels happy. Soon enough, you are filled with this happy pink color.

The same goes for negative thoughts. Think of negative thoughts as a black color. The more black you pour into the water, the harder it is to see any of the other colors. The black begins to muddle everything, and it becomes hard to see anything but the black. This is what happens when you give your negative thoughts power and focus on them. They grow and grow until your whole mind becomes overtaken by them, making it hard to change your thoughts to anything different.

But the thing is, when the first little dropper of black came into the water, there was an opportunity to allow the clear water to disperse the little bit of black until it was clear again. We always have this choice when negative thoughts come. We can pay them no attention and allow our minds to become clear again, or we can focus on the negative thoughts until our minds are completely overtaken by them.

This is exactly why there is no need to obsess over or fear our thoughts. As I mentioned, when people learn that our thoughts create our reality, they feel terrified of any thought that comes in if it isn't positive. They can't stop ruminating about the thoughts they are having.

I hope this helps you understand that the thoughts that are coming in and simply going have absolutely no power over your reality. It doesn't matter why they came; your brain will think up a ton of different thoughts for no reason at all. You aren't a weirdo or a bad person because your brain crafted up an odd thought. If you allow it to pass, it will pass.

If a thought shakes me up, I gently remind myself that it's not a thought that reflects me. I say something like, "That isn't a thought I want more of," and I imagine the black disappearing into the clear water.

If it keeps coming up over and over again, it might not be a bad idea to take to your journal. If certain thoughts keep returning it is because they are old patterns ready to be healed and released. For instance, maybe you keep having the thought that you will never find the right partner. It comes up and you try to let it go, but then it resurfaces.

This is a great opportunity to get in touch with your emotions, and your thought patterns, and allow yourself to get to the root of why those thoughts are coming up in the first place. Oftentimes, these thoughts are a result of an experience that caused your brain to hold this belief.

117

These beliefs are called your "limiting beliefs." Limiting beliefs are those that you hold deep within you and negatively affect your thoughts, feelings, and behaviors—most of the time without your knowledge.

If you take a look at your most common thought patterns, behaviors, and things that keep recurring in your life, you will be able to gain insight into what your limiting beliefs are.[7]

The importance of our belief system

When you think about your beliefs, you probably think about your political stances, religious views, or your values and morals. However, your beliefs go much deeper than this. Before the age of seven, your brain is a sponge absorbing everything from your environment. During this time, your brain is molding your belief system. As a little kid, you may have some idea about religion or values from what your parents teach you or what you overhear, but the beliefs you are creating have more to do with how you see yourself, people, and the world around you. The strongest beliefs you hold over time become your "core beliefs." The core beliefs you created are extremely impactful and will dictate how you operate daily for the rest of your life—until you change them. Although everyone's beliefs are different, we *all* have them.

The scientific reason our belief system is so important is because it is our brain's map for creating the reality we experience. According to *Psychology Today*, "Beliefs create a cognitive lens through which you interpret the events of your world, and this lens serves as a selective filter through which you sift the environment for evidence that matches up with what you believe to be true."[1]

Unfortunately, some of the beliefs we hold are unhealthy and do not benefit us. And, like healthy beliefs, your brain is *still* looking for evidence to confirm these beliefs as true through that cognitive lens. These are called our limiting beliefs.

This is exactly why things show up in your world as a pattern. If you believe and assume everything goes wrong for you, your brain's filtering system is primed by this belief to look for confirmation that this is true. When your brain does this, it shuts down other competing neural networks, making it hard to see any evidence that debunks your belief. If you believe you always meet the best people, that everything flows easily for you in life, and you are a confident and respected person, you *will* see more of that show up in your reality.

The root of much of our continuous suffering within our minds is a limiting belief that created a story in our memory. A story that was taught to us through the harshness of the world. Through this harshness, this story became our own and a member of our belief system. It's no wonder when someone suffers often, it becomes ingrained in them in some way. For some, it's all they know. But these stories were never meant to be ours forever. Although our story is what shapes the path of our life and turns us into the person we're meant to be, the parts of our story that hold us back from reaching our highest potential are meant to be undone and rewritten.

Think about something in life you have mastered. Something you feel proud of, where you say to yourself, "Easy, I could do that in my sleep." You have mastered it to the point where it has become second nature. Maybe you are amazing at remaining calm in any situation, you can nail any public speaking event, or you can start a conversation with anyone. You've mastered it because of the amount of times you have done it, and it built a healthy belief within your belief system. Your brain knows it, predicts it, and completes it on autopilot. But since it is something positive, it's happily part of your story. You don't question it. It's there, and you are proud of it.

I want you to think of an area of your life where you struggle and have for a long time. You feel like no matter how hard you try, you simply cannot master it or get past it, it just *keeps* happening time and time again. We can use the example of friendship. Let's say you have had countless friends, but no matter what, the friendship ends in a huge blowout fight where you're left yelling, "See, I'm not good enough for anyone!" What I'm going to tell you, you might not like to hear. Stick with me though, as it'll make sense in the end.

You feel you have not mastered this story because it always ends in something negative, right? But this isn't as true as you may think. You *have* mastered this story.

Why? Because the story is *always* the same. Your brain knows it, predicts it, and completes it just as easily as it did the very thing you have mastered that you feel so proud of.

So much of what we do is unconscious action—we don't even *realize* we are doing it. Our brain is guiding us in a way where we unconsciously say, do, and feel things that align with this story and keep it going. The story your brain keeps replaying, which leaves you feeling defeated every single time has nothing to do with you doing anything consciously wrong, it's simply due to the story under the surface.

We *all* have stories under the surface, and if we don't look for them and uncover what they are, our brains will continue to memorize and replay them. Our brains

120

don't care about what we humans believe to be "positive" or "negative." It only cares about predictability. *Predictability is safety for the human brain.*

Therefore, if the experiences you had in your childhood led you to believe that love is conditional and everyone always leaves you, that becomes part of the predictable story in your brain. You learned it as well as you learned the skill you are proud of. So before your next relationship even starts, your brain is unconsciously looking to make the story that everyone always leaves you to become true. Naturally, you will seek out and attract people who will fulfill that story. Until you discover these stories, otherwise called your limiting beliefs, they will run your life. Do you ever wonder why some people you know tend to have the worst luck? Or the best? The truth is, it's not luck at all. It's the stories the person holds within their subconscious mind.

I want to put a disclaimer here before we continue, which I feel is very important:

No one deserved the negative stories created for them as children. No one deserved the outcomes that came from them having to carry those stories with them their entire lives. But when we understand our brains are wired this way and will continue to be wired this way, we can be empowered to change those old stories. We had no power when we unconsciously took on those stories as little kids and teenagers. Now that we are adults, we can take back our power and discover what has been controlling our lives for so long. So, although I know this may not be a comfortable lesson to learn, you must rewrite your new narrative. The most successful people in the world have allowed their difficult pasts to empower them, they did not become victims of it. You deserve to do the same.

I am not going to "everything happens for a reason" you to death when it comes to the difficult things you have gone through in your lifetime. The bottom line is, no matter how you choose to view it, whether you can see how the difficulties helped your future unfold or not, you don't deserve to go through it. But the fact is that you are in a place in your life where you are looking to move into the future as your best self. Doing so will mean there will be past parts of you to let go of, forgive, and *allow yourself* to heal from.

As much as our life traumas often impacted us greatly and shaped a huge portion of our lives whether for good or bad, we have to choose to allow ourselves to heal and change. To detach our identity from all of it and not remain a victim of past circumstances.

121

There is power in reminding yourself that all of those things that caused you to struggle over and over again are based on the stories you tell yourself. Up until now, you believed these stories were absolute truths about you. When you see that they aren't, that they hold no truth and can be changed at any moment, you gain personal power like you've never had before.

Of course, we have to understand that things not working out for us or something going wrong is *not always* due to limiting beliefs. There are plenty of reasons things don't work out. Consider the concept we discussed about things happening on a different timeline than we expected. The concept we are discussing has to do with the *repeating patterns* that keep occurring in your life that you can't get a grasp on and why they won't go right. However, when acknowledging the science of our brains, we can see the beliefs we hold *do* have a huge impact on our reality.

I'll share with you some examples of common stories people carry with them so you can understand the way this affects every single person.

A man loses everything. Let's say he was a very successful man who had all the fancy cars, cool houses, and flashy things. He always was in a relationship. He lost everything and completely closed himself off to finding love. He feels unworthy of love because he now has "nothing" to offer: no fancy cars, money, or a big home. His story was that if he was able to have all the fanciest material things, he was valuable as a lover. His self-worth was tied to what he had. So when he lost all of these things, he no longer felt valuable as a partner. Of course, he is inherently worthy of love and can provide a partner so much more if he knows how to: emotionally support, show affection, be a good partner, etc. But since his story tells him he is not valuable unless he can provide material possessions, he *believes* he is unworthy. Somewhere along the way, the people in his life showed him or told him that a man's worth lies in his ability to provide.

This story is all too common in our society. There is nothing wrong with a man wanting to provide, but he must have self-worth coming from a deeper place. Where if he could no longer provide, he would still feel worthy as a human being. Material wealth can always be fleeting. Deep self-worth is something that can create true resilience through life's difficulties. When he was unaware that he was being run by this narrative, his actions reflected it. He became closed off and felt unworthy of love. When he became aware of this narrative he shifted it to one that empowered him. He is worthy of love simply because of who he is, that he is a great man at his core and able to provide emotionally for his partner, and he understands that is enough of a reason to be loved. Now, he can rebuild his life.

122

A young girl has been objectified from a young age. Classmates and people around her have been making suggestive comments about her body since she was 12. At this young age, she, like everyone else, just wanted to feel accepted. She realized when she got this attention it made her feel good, important even. But no one ever noticed her for anything else. No one paid attention to how she helped others, how smart she was in school, or her athletic achievements. Eventually, the story she began to carry without realizing it was that her worth lies in her appearance. She felt like if she didn't look perfect all the time she was unworthy of love. She felt she had to uphold this certain appearance that allowed the story to continue; appearance = attention and feeling important. This affected her relationships and entire adult life until she realized it. She felt if her appearance fluctuated at all: weight gain, acne, aging, not wearing makeup, she wouldn't be worthy of love. Because of this, she unconsciously attracted partners who cared only about the surface and didn't care to get to know her. They belittled her for fluctuations in her appearance and their love was conditional to that. This further continued the story that her worth only lied in how she looked. When she became aware of this story, she was able to understand that she only believed it due to the way she grew up. She realized there was no truth to her story, that she was only worthy of love if she looked a certain way. She was worthy because of who she was—she always held the inherent worthiness of love. This allowed her to create a secure relationship with herself. So now, even if anyone tried to make her feel less than beautiful, she still felt she was enough. She began to attract partners who saw and accepted her for who she was as a person. She accepted herself in all forms, and in turn her story changed. Her story empowered her to love herself no matter what.

Fear is another big story that runs people's lives in some way or another. Let's take a woman who wants to start her own business. Her parents were ordinary people who worked 9-5. No one encouraged her to live her dreams. In fact, she was told she wouldn't be able to do it. She was told it was too expensive, would take too much time, was too hard, and that she wasn't enough of a leader. This became her story. As you can see, it was never hers to begin with. It was the people's story around her that was imprinted onto her. Her story began as a dreamer but eventually led to her settling. She settled for a comfortable job she didn't like but paid the bills. She settled for a nice partner, but she wasn't in love with them. She always felt like something was missing from her life, so she was never really happy. Eventually, she realized it was because she adopted this story from others around her. She never lived for herself or did things she wanted to do. She did things others expected of her, and she adopted their beliefs along with it. Once she realized this, she found the courage to step outside of the world of comfort she had created in her reality. She started trying to build her business. She failed a few times, but each time she learned more. She knew all she had to do was keep going. She adopted a new story that aligned with her best self. She believed in herself no matter what. She knew she could do anything, and even if she messed up, she knew she was still good enough to keep going.

These are just a few of the common stories that affect people's lives without them realizing it. The stories get to change. Your story gets to be different. Ready to learn how to change yours?

Action steps you can take:

The first step to changing your limiting beliefs and your story is becoming aware of what your current mindset is. Maybe you know you struggle with overthinking or negative self-talk, but you don't understand where those thoughts come from. This is where we can begin to uncover that. [5,7]

Begin to consciously notice what thoughts are running through your mind throughout the day: The most important time to tune into your thoughts is when you are worried about something, angry, frustrated, something bad happens, you feel impatient, or someone upsets you. Pay attention to all the little moments and what you say to yourself when you look in the mirror, when you make a mistake, or when nothing seems to be going your way. All of this is important. This is a great time to further what we did in the "feeling difficult emotions" chapter. Your homework was to begin to notice your emotions and your reactions to them. I asked you to simply begin the process by creating that awareness. Maybe now you have a bit more awareness of what your reactions to your emotions are: retreating to your bedroom when you feel depressed, being unable to stop talking when you're anxious, self-criticizing when you are angry, etc.

Whatever your findings were, you can take it a step further. What did you think about when you felt those emotions? When you are depressed, for example, what do you say to yourself? Common thoughts could be, "I'll never be where I want to be," "I can never do anything right," or "I am a failure." Have a brain dump section in your phone notes app or use this workbook as your safe space to write if you prefer. Write it all down. Every thought that is significant to you. Every self-critical thought. Every thought that doesn't feel good. Look out for thoughts that start with, "I am…" "I never…" or, "I always…" These types of thoughts are dictators of what your patterns are. Do this as much as you can for at least a week straight (the longer, the better) to see what you can learn about yourself. Take a break from this book if you want to and just focus on that, whatever feels right.

An example for your workbook/phone notes: I feel sad→ my reaction to that feeling is isolating in my room → some of the thoughts I am having include I am never going to amount to anything, I never know what to do, I always make the worst decisions, I am such a mess.

When you are ready to continue after completing the first step, you can get started on the next one.

The second step to figuring out your limiting beliefs is finding out what your most common thought patterns are. When we become aware of our thoughts, emotions, and our reactions to them, we will see recurring ones.

How to recognize your patterns: Have handy the page in this workbook or your phone notes app where you brain dumped all your thoughts from the past week. Write down the thoughts from your findings on the blank page below.

You can make something in your notebook that looks like this:

LIMITING BELIEFS

1 I am never enough for anyone

2 I can't do anything right so nothing works out for me

2 I'm never going to amount to anything

1 I should just cut this relationship off because they'll leave me anyways

3 I'm not doing enough, everyone around me is doing better than me

1 I'll never find anyone who accepts me for me

2 I always give up on everything I try to do

3 I'm not smart enough compared to others my age to get the job

3 I'm such a failure for my age, I should have accomplished more by now

LIMITING BELIEFS:

From looking at your diagram, you can figure out what your most common limiting beliefs are. Even if you had tons of different thoughts written down, you can find common themes within all of them.

Common examples of limiting beliefs about the self could be: "I never get anything I want," "I'm not smart enough," "I am undeserving of good things," "I am not worth paying attention to," "I am unlovable," or, "I am shy, and my voice shouldn't be heard."

About other people: "It's difficult to form relationships with others," "Most people are out to get me," "No one likes being around me," "It's not safe to speak my mind to other people," "People aren't safe to trust," or, "People will hurt me or leave me."

About the world: "Success is hard to come by," "There isn't enough abundance in the world for all of us," "Life is only getting worse," "The world is unfair," "Life is hard and unpredictable," or, "The world is bad and unjust."

Looking at the example of the diagram I made above of all the different thoughts that came up, these are what I would conclude could be this person's most apparent limiting beliefs:

#2: I am incapable of achieving what I desire.
#1: I am unworthy of love.
#3: I am inadequate compared to others.

From here, we can break these limiting beliefs down even further. To begin, choose one of your limiting beliefs. Refer to the example below to help guide you. I'll use the limiting belief, "I am incapable of achieving what I desire."

Now that you can pinpoint this limiting belief, think about your life. How has this limiting belief shown up as a pattern throughout your life?

It seems like every time I try to put effort into something I want, it doesn't work. I try to implement new habits, and I can never get them to stick. I failed out of the courses I signed up for. I try to go on dates with people and they always go terribly, and I seem to always make the decision that gets me further away from what I want in life.

Where did you get this belief from? When do you think you first started having these thoughts that reflect it? Did something happen when you were young to cause you to believe this? Are these thoughts your voice, or are they someone else's voice from the past?

I remember having thoughts like this as young as eight. I would get home from practice and my parents would yell at me for how horrible I played and remind me I'd never amount to anything in the sport. I'd quit the sport later on because I played worse and worse, even if I loved it. These thoughts of being incapable came from the voice of my parents.

When these thoughts come up, how do you feel?

When I think these thoughts about being incapable, I feel a sense of dread. I feel like I'm stuck in a never-ending loop of starting and quickly quitting or losing what I started. I feel ashamed, anxious, and angry that I can't seem to achieve anything.

When you start to feel all of those emotions you just described, how does it affect your actions?

It paralyzes me. I don't push forward or try again, I stop trying new things altogether, and I often settle for things I don't want because I don't feel like I could achieve anything better.

If this limiting belief came from a person or situation outside of yourself, was it *ever* true? Was it someone's *opinion* you believed was a fact? Or did the experience cause you to believe it as a fact, but it never actually was?

Now that I think of it, it was the opinion of my parents that they put onto me. I was only a kid, so I took it as truth. I believed everything they told me as fact, so I took it on as one of my self-beliefs. The experiences I had afterward caused me to further see it as evidence, so I never knew any different.

If you were able to drop this belief today, who would you be without it? What would you accomplish? How would you feel? What thoughts would you have instead?

I would feel so much better about myself! I would finally feel like I could achieve what I wanted. I would make progress because I wouldn't give up on myself so easily, and I would be able to try new things without fearing my ability to do it well. I would feel free, motivated, and much happier. I would think thoughts that inspire me such as, "I am capable of achieving anything I put my mind to," or, "I always accomplish what I set out to because I keep going no matter what."

Let's replace this limiting belief with a new one. A great way to do this is to find the opposite of what this belief means but start with something that feels believable to you. The more believable the new belief, the easier it will be to implement it into your mindset. For example: I am the worst at conversation with new people: I am getting consistently better at conversation with new people, and I am always improving.

I am incapable of achieving what I desire→I am capable of achieving anything I put my mind to because I always keep going.

Now that you can pinpoint this limiting belief, think about your life. How has this limiting belief shown up as a pattern throughout your life?

_____

_____

_____

_____

_____

_____

_____

_____

_____

_____

Where did you get this belief from? When do you think you first started having these thoughts that reflect it? Did something happen when you were young to cause you to believe this? Are these thoughts your voice, or are they someone else's voice from the past?

_____

_____

_____

_____

_____

_____

_____

When these thoughts come up, how do you feel?

_____

_____

_____

_____

_____

_____

_____

_____

When you start to feel all of those emotions you just described, how does it affect your actions?

_____

_____

_____

_____

_____

_____

_____

_____

_____

_____

_____

If this limiting belief came from a person or situation outside of yourself, was it _ever_ true? Was it someone's _opinion_ you believed was a fact? Or did the experience cause you to believe it as a fact, but it never actually was?

_____

_____

_____

_____

_____

_____

_____

_____

_____

_____

If you were able to drop this belief today, who would you be without it? What would you accomplish? How would you feel? What thoughts would you have instead?

_____

_____

_____

_____

_____

_____

_____

_____

_____

_____

_____

Let's replace this limiting belief with a new one. A great way to do this is to find the opposite of what this belief means but start with something that feels believable to you. The more believable the new belief, the easier it will be to implement it into your mindset.

Working through our limiting beliefs allows us to expose the false nature of the belief. When you break down the belief and see it for what it is, you can see it was never true about you. Contrary to what you may have believed up until now, you are *not* all of the negative things you believed you were. Now that you understand this, you can create a new vision for your future—one that reflects the version of you that you want to be, not who you thought you were or who you thought you had to be.

Doing exercises like this will allow you to learn how to build self-awareness and resiliency for the future. You will be able to reflect on life's challenges and have a deeper understanding of your actions so you can seek the necessary wisdom from the situation to move forward. You won't linger and become stuck in a victim mentality when life hands you lemons.

Who is your ideal self?

Allowing yourself to dream will help you have something to work toward and remind you why you are doing this in the first place.

To start, you are going to take inventory of your current life.

Identify what you currently like and dislike about your current situation. Highlight everything you are doing well and want to continue, including qualities you love about yourself, habits that serve you, and relationships you want to continue to grow. Highlight what you need to work on, habits to let go of, and relationships that drain you. Do a complete life overhaul and get clear about what is staying and what is going in this new chapter of your life.

_____

_____

_____

_____

_____

_____

_____

_____

_____

_____

_____

_____

_____

_____

_____

_____

_____

_____

_____

_____

_____

_____

After you take inventory of all the things you do and do not like about your life, you will begin to imagine who the best version of you is. This is something you can do *without* having any clue what your career will be or what you want to accomplish in life. From the limiting beliefs chapter, we learned that we may have thought we had to be a certain way for the rest of our lives, but that we are free to change at any time. You get to choose who you want to be, no matter if you believe it's possible right now or not. So dream big and allow yourself to consider the fact that you *can* embody any quality you wish to. You *can* have the confidence to be the person you always wanted to be even if it seemed too far out of reach. Answer the questions in your workbook below to help you:

Who is the ideal version of yourself—your "best" self? What is that version of you like? What qualities do you embody? How would you dress daily? How would you act? What would your daily life be like? How would you treat people? How would people treat you? How would you show up in your relationships? How would you spend your money? How much money would you have? What would your health be like? What would your workout routine be if you could go to any gym or fitness class you wanted? What types of groceries would you buy if you didn't have to worry about a budget? What would you prioritize? What are your values? What mark do you want to leave on the world?

_____

_____

_____

_____

_____

_____

_____

_____

_____

_____

_____

_____

_____

_____

_____

The next step is to "why" yourself like crazy. Why do you want these things you just described? There is *always* a deeper meaning to why you want the things you do. Usually, it's an emotion you are looking to feel. For example, you may want designer clothing to help you feel more confident. You may want to feel more confident because then you could set better boundaries in your relationships. If you were more confident you'd be able to get your dream job, etc. Figure out the root of why you want particular things and decide which emotions you are looking to feel based on the things you desire in your dream life.

_____

_____

_____

_____

_____

_____

_____

_____

_____

_____

_____

_____

_____

_____

Michelle Lynn Johnson

The reason you want all of those things in your dream life needs to come back to YOU and only you. Your reason for wanting things should not come from a superficial place or be motivated by other people. Think about this, it would be amazing to have money to help other people. This is a great reason to want more of it. Still, though, there's an emotion at the root of wanting to help people. Your true reason for having more money may be the fulfillment that comes from being able to help others. If you want certain things to impress other people, prove yourself to other people, or because you feel pressured to have them, these aren't sustainable desires. These desires won't be authentic to you. Remember, having authentic dreams will allow you to feel energized and excited about life. Dreams that do not feel authentic to you will result in quick burnout.

The most efficient way to turn your dreams into reality is to understand the emotion behind your desires and begin finding ways to create more of those emotions in your life now. Act as if you are already living your dream reality by actively deciding to step into the emotions you desire.

The reason this method is so powerful is the same as why visualization in meditation is so powerful: our brains cannot differentiate between what is real and what is imagined.

When acting as if you are living your dream reality, figure out when you felt the emotions you want to feel more of in your past. You have felt confident, free, or passionate before if you know what it feels like to want more of it. As you experience more of this emotion, you will step into a new reality—one where you consistently embody all that you desire.

If you feel free when you dance or when you go on a car ride listening to music with the windows down, then do that! If you feel confident when you dress up, do that! If you feel alive when you go for a run, go for more runs! Choosing little actions like those instead of reverting to your old ways will be the difference between staying the same and living your dreams.

The next part of this concept is to understand what it means to have your actions be in harmony with your desires. This is why it is critical to do an inventory of your current life and see what habits and actions you need to kick to the curb. One of the most difficult things for people to do is act a certain way when they don't feel that way yet. For example, if one of your desires is to feel calmer, but you are still actively saying, "I'm an anxious person, I can never feel peaceful." Affirming out loud that you could never achieve being a calm person doesn't harmonize with the passionate excitement you feel about learning to feel calmer. An action that's in alignment with your excitement about your new journey toward calmness would be meditating, taking yoga classes, going for walks in nature, or journaling out your anxious thoughts.

Another common example of this is if you desire a new relationship, but you're dwelling on your past relationships. You might constantly tell people, "Yeah, well, I've been burned many times before. People always treat me terribly." Or maybe you are going on dates, but you spend the entire time talking about a past partner. Your *actions* are what matters, not just stating your desires. You can say you want something until you are blue in the face, but if your actions say something else, you will keep seeing the results from the current actions you are taking.

This is why it is so important to build self-awareness. To understand what actions we have been taking and why we have been doing them. To learn about ourselves on a deeper level because **we all do this.** We all have desires that we can't seem to bring into reality because we are in our own way. Oftentimes, without any realization, it is our actions building a wall between us and what we want.

I hope you find this to be exciting. To know that a small change in action can and will cause big results. All it takes is getting clear on what you desire, tweaking your habits to reflect those desires, and ditching the actions that are keeping you stuck.

Creating a vision when you don't yet know what's next

It's unhelpful to tell young adults to set super specific goals when they don't have any idea what they want to do with their lives. Oftentimes, the only sense of knowing what they want next comes from what society tells them they *should* want after graduation. Many people will ask, "So, what's the next step?"

With that comes a lot of pressure to have a "good" answer. An answer that doesn't make you feel embarrassed or behind. An answer that doesn't cause them to give you a look of pity.

I want you to understand that starting to make changes in your life **does not** require you to know what your next step will be. There is so much pressure during this time of your life to figure it out and it is discouraging for many graduates. The truth is that you may not know the next step right away. It may take a lot of trial and error before you have a real sense of what you want. You may change your mind over and over again throughout the years, and that's more than okay!

When you think about setting goals postgrad, you probably think of something like this:

Goals:

1. Become a manager at my job by June.
2. Get a raise and make $100,000 by the time I'm 24.
3. Purchase a home by 30.
4. Have three kids by 27.
5. Visit ten countries by 25.

What do you notice about the *way* these goals are set?

They are set on a **timeline.** Some are more guaranteed than others. For example, there's more of a chance you can guarantee to visit ten countries by 25 or buy a home by 30 than you can have three kids by 27 or become a manager.

How can you set helpful goals when you don't quite know what you want? Essentially it's a shot in the dark and hoping it sticks, but not having any idea where it's going to land or why you want it to land there in the first place.

Let's refresh what we learned in the first part of this book about having patience for the unknown and why it's okay to not know what is next. Both of those sections talk about how much of our lives is out of our control and entirely unpredictable. Remember, we might believe we know what is best for us at the moment based on logic, but what we want based on this logic might not be what the universe has in store for us. So, it might not happen on the timeline we set because it was never meant to.

We cannot force ourselves onto the timeline that we *think* is right for us. When we set a timeline for when things *have* to happen for us, we create attachments to those outcomes. When we are attached to outcomes, it is hard to accept change. It is difficult to imagine a life outside of the rigid structures we created.

When you create these rigid structures, you are confining yourself to just a few possibilities and limiting your growth potential. Imagine putting a goldfish in a small bowl. Scientifically, it's proven that goldfish grow based on the size of their environment. When one is put in a small bowl with poor water quality, the goldfish remains small (just a few inches long) and can't grow to its full potential. But, in a pond or lake, goldfish grow the entirety of their lives. The goldfish can end up as big as a football when there are no confinements for them.

This is the difference between setting goals on a timeline and creating a vision for your life.

When you create a vision for your life that reflects the kind of person you want to grow into, the emotions you want to feel, and the impact you want to leave on the world, the possibilities are truly *endless.* There are no limits and no attachments, and the energy of remaining open can open doors that you didn't even know were options. Doors that hold things you couldn't even have dreamed up but are so wildly aligned with who you are.

So instead, a great place to start if you don't quite know what you want yet is to create a vision for who you want to be and what you want your impact on the world to be and decide which daily habits will help you accomplish these things.

For example:

1. I want to feel present in my daily life and with those I have relationships with so I can build deeper connections with others, and myself, and feel like I am fully living my now.

Habits that reflect achieving this goal:
- Daily meditation (scientifically proven to help create presence in your life and a deeper connection with yourself.
- Practice active listening in conversations with others daily: listening to understand and not respond (this will create deeper connections with others and allow you to practice being present in the moment).
- Incorporate a highly stimulating hobby (working out is a great one), something that requires your full attention and makes sure you are completely present.

2. I want to make the world a better place. I am open to ways that I can do that, but my goal is to do something every day to leave a meaningful impact on others.

Habits:
- Spreading kindness by writing someone a kind note, offering a genuine smile, buying someone flowers, or complimenting someone.
- Being of service to people in your life: offering a listening ear, going out of your way to make their life easier, reminding people how loved and appreciated they are.
- Make social media content that inspires others and is a bright light within a surplus of negative media people have to consume.

3. Change my mindset so my thoughts reflect the person I want to be. I want to be more of an optimist and learn how to speak more kindly to myself.

Habits:
- Journaling daily all of the negative thoughts that come up and work to get to the root of where they came from.
- Ask yourself every day, "What would be the best-case scenario?"

- Doing inner child healing exercises to help you learn why you are so critical of yourself and heal the parts of you that are wounded from the past.

Creating a vision that is mission-based and implementing daily habits that go along with these goals will allow you to actively create a life that goes along with your mission or your "why" for being here on Earth. You won't worry about remaining on a certain timeline or shame yourself if you don't accomplish what you thought you would. You will allow your life to unfold exactly how it is meant to because you are taking actions that align with your vision. You will be able to part with the need to control.

Think about it like this: there are many situations in life we wish we had control over. We try to insert ourselves and manipulate outcomes because we can't handle the feeling of not having control. Imagine you are trying to get a new job. You apply, get an interview, attend the interview, and send a follow-up email thanking the employer for their time. You REALLY want this job. However, it's been a few days, and you still haven't heard back. You took *all* the right actions already, but still, you feel the need to try to control the outcome because you want it so badly. You're tempted to email another time because the waiting phase is so uncomfortable, and the idea of rejection is killing you. However, sending another email will not change the speediness of their decision or get them to want to hire you. Since you already took the right steps, it's important to trust that if it's the right job for you, you'll get it, and there is no need to go overboard during the waiting process. Let go of the need to control what will happen next since there is no way to control the hiring manager in this situation.

The same goes for life. If we create a vision for our lives and are consistently taking actions aligned with this vision, we can feel confident that things are happening in the way they are meant to. It is *enough* to show up daily and take these little actions. We don't need to go overboard to manipulate outcomes or try to force things into happening. Your path will always be exactly what it is meant to be, even if the path you are on feels uncertain. We aren't meant to always know what is next on our path.

I could never have dreamt up or predicted any of the events that took place for me postgrad. There wasn't a world where I ever thought I wouldn't have gotten a corporate job after college. Never in my life did I think I would write a book. I never thought helping people through postgrad transition was something I would be so passionate about. I never thought I would travel the world instead of getting married and having kids in my mid-twenties.

146

But, remaining open and giving up the need to control everything allowed my life to unfold how it was meant to. I was meant to do all of this all along, I just didn't know until it happened.

There is nothing wrong with having specific goals for what you are trying to achieve if you know for certain it is what you want. Some people have known from an early age what they want to accomplish in life, and in that case, all the power to you in working towards that.

The bottom line is, though, that a huge portion of young adults have no idea what they want yet because they are still developing who they are. My objective here is to provide a solution for those who are stuck in that area.

I was there, too, when I was freshly graduated. I didn't learn this right away, but when I finally did, it changed the way I felt about life in my 20s. It took the pressure off and allowed me to take it day by day knowing I was taking the action needed to create the life I wanted to live.

You will not crash and burn, fail, or be a disappointment if you let go of the need to predict your life. Decide who you want to be, what your life mission is, and how you want to feel, and you will be *well* on your way to living a life aligned with what is in your heart.

Michelle Lynn Johnson

Building a relationship with *you*

I have talked a lot in the first part of this book about the importance of building a relationship with yourself during this time of your life. What does it mean to "Build a relationship with yourself?"

Consider what it's like when you build a relationship with a new person. To create a strong relationship with someone new, there are a few things that need to happen before you consider it to be a healthy relationship. You need to work on building trust between the two of you, you need to take the time to get to know each other on a deep level so you can support each other in the way you both need, and you need to be able to work through the hard moments together in a healthy way.

This is *exactly* what you need to do with yourself. The reality is a lot of us have or have had an unhealthy relationship with ourselves at one time or another. When your relationship with yourself needs some work, you might: harshly criticize and judge yourself, shame yourself when you aren't productive, force perfectionist standards upon yourself, only make decisions after asking other people for advice, or do things only to please or get acceptance from others.

There are so many things we aren't taught to learn about ourselves. The things I have learned about myself that have altered my life the most were things I didn't realize could affect me or were affecting me. Like learning what happens in your body and brain when something in the external world triggers you to get upset or angry. Learning what repeating thoughts you have and where those thoughts came from in the first place. Knowing what stories and beliefs you hold about the world and yourself that you have carried with you since you were a little child. Knowing what helps you become grounded again when you are having a freak-out moment. Knowing what types of personalities you get along with best in a friendship or romantic relationship and knowing what types of behaviors from others cause you stress or anxiety. Understanding what your worst traits are just as well as knowing your good qualities, so you can understand how to treat others better.

I will share with you exactly how you can get started on this so you, too, can create a strong and secure relationship with yourself going into this next chapter of your life.

Learning to cultivate self-love:

We hear so much about self-love in simplified terms. You have probably heard someone say, "You have to love yourself before you can love anyone else."

If you google images of "self-love" I bet you would see countless images with quotes just like that one. But what does it *entail* to love yourself? And why is it so common for people to struggle to do so, to the point where it has to be plastered all over the internet so people can be reminded?

The reason self-love is so important is that without it, we look to the external world to help us feel loved, whole, and accepted. The difference between getting this validation from the external world and creating validation internally is that when it comes from the external world, you will *never* be satisfied. You will always need more and more and more. You will rely on receiving more compliments, receiving more praise, and seeking more confirmation that you are enough. You will make decisions based on what will get you the most attention and praise from this external source, not based on what you desire. Eventually, you will become disconnected from your authentic desires because you become too engulfed only in doing what would "look" good to others in hopes that external sources will keep filling the void inside of you.

Creating deep inner love and security within yourself is what allows you to become a person who can follow your desires and step into a life that is perfectly aligned with who you are. You will not feel the need to look to outside sources to tell you you are making the right choices. You will be able to face adversity without crumbling because when someone or something pops up in your path trying to knock your self-esteem, you will be secure enough in yourself to know you are enough without their approval. You will be able to show up for yourself on your bad days because you care about yourself and your future enough to push through feeling uncomfortable.

Everyone thinks self-love is all rainbows and butterflies, baths and face masks. *It doesn't always look like that.* Self-love is much deeper than that and doesn't always feel as good as we think it should. For example, think of a time you had to make a decision that broke your heart, but you knew it was the right thing to do so you did it anyway. A lot of the time that is what self-love looks like. Choosing yourself by

150

choosing the right decision instead of the one that feels the best or the easiest. That is what it means to love yourself and put self-love into action. Loving yourself means you respect yourself enough to make hard decisions. You honor yourself even if it feels uncomfortable.

One of the best ways to explain this concept is by considering our relationships with other people. This is a path most of us will cross at some point in our lives. Whether it is with family, friends, or romantic partners, there will be a time when you have to express a need for a change in their behavior. The infamous "boundary setting." The reason why I use this as an example to explain self-love is that doing this requires you to step out of your comfort zone in the name of making sure your needs are met, and you are putting yourself first. Setting boundaries with people is often met with retaliation. They might cross that boundary every time they get the chance if you give them the opportunity. Instead of backing down and letting people step all over the boundaries you set, stand firm on your expectations. *This is an act of self-love.* Yes, it doesn't feel good when someone you love is pushing back on the boundaries you are trying so hard to set, but not giving in shows you respect yourself. Giving in shows the other person that you don't respect yourself enough to stand up to them, and they can walk all over you. This also confirms in your brain that another person's comfort is more important than your love for yourself. Hard choices such as setting boundaries fall in the category of what it means to truly love yourself.

Self-love happens *over time* when you continuously keep promises to yourself, when you show up for yourself, when you are firm on the boundaries you set with others, and when you can accept yourself as you are, fully and completely.

You need to accept yourself on the bad days just as much as the good days. You must accept the parts of yourself that may not be as "desirable" as other parts. When you accept yourself completely, you are mastering a big part of self-love.

Unconditionally loving yourself means you don't have certain conditions where you love yourself. If you love yourself conditionally, that means you will fall apart on a bad day or when you make a mistake. You will shame yourself for being human, your very essence. So start now. Go on this journey with yourself. Decide to try every day to show up and have compassion for yourself no matter the circumstances. Showing yourself compassion and grace will go a long way in this life, as no one is perfect.

I have had to check myself many times on my journey, and I'm sure I will have to do so in the future. There have been plenty of times when I noticed myself speaking harshly within my inner monologue during times in my life when my body didn't look the way I wanted it to, when I was struggling to be productive, or when I got off track on my habits. I had to recognize that if I am not able to love and accept myself when I am struggling or when I don't look according to the high standards I have set, then I am not loving myself at all. Because inevitably, as humans, we will always fluctuate. If we set standards for ourselves that require being perfect all the time to receive love from ourselves, we will ultimately fail to live up to them.

You cannot reject yourself and expect to find self-love at the same time (yup, been there, tried that). If you do this, you are declaring that you can only love yourself once you change something about yourself. If you decide that you love yourself when you land an awesome job, but that you hate yourself for getting fired from the last one, your love for yourself is conditional.

The journey of accepting yourself takes time, but it is one of the most important gifts you can give yourself in this life. Especially in a world that has harsh beauty standards and ideas of what success needs to look like, it can be difficult to accept yourself as you are.

When those conditions include you only accepting and loving yourself when you do good things, you will spend much of your time during your short lifetime rejecting yourself. We discussed how the low points of life and the heavy emotions humans feel are inevitable. We cannot live a life where we only experience perfection all the time because our imperfect humanness is our very essence. Imperfection is not a negative quality, it's simply a *human* quality.

You deserve to shower yourself with compassion on the days you make mistakes. You deserve to be the one who has your back when someone rejects you, reminding yourself you are still enough. You deserve to love yourself so much that when people in your life do not treat you with that same love back, you can stand up for yourself knowing you deserve better.

Self-rejection will keep you feeling stuck in life. You can't possibly be aligned with your best self and live your most authentic life when you are rejecting the parts that are authentically you. You deserve to be authentically you. And the thing is, it might just take becoming aware of how you are treating yourself. Likely, you don't even realize you are holding yourself to impossible standards or not allowing yourself to be human, but when you do recognize it, it will be much easier to show yourself that love.

Chapter summary for putting self-love into action:

-Showing up for yourself when you don't want to
-Making difficult decisions and sticking behind them even when it's hard
-Standing firm on your boundaries with both yourself and others
-Not setting unrealistic conditions under which you can love yourself
-Allowing yourself to listen to your intuition and your body to better give yourself what you need instead of listening to other people
-Giving yourself grace and showing yourself compassion even on your worst days

The most critical step for beginning your journey:

Within this journey of change and self-evolution, you will require the need for extra nurturing. And no, I don't mean from others. You will need to nurture your spirit during this time of change.

There will be heaviness in this journey. Within all of the self-honesty, vulnerability, courageous action, and willful pushes into the unknown, you will need to wrap yourself in a blanket of love, compassion, grace, and acceptance quite often.

I would argue that a journey of change *without* incorporating this step is a journey that will be short-lived. Your battery to move forward will quickly run empty, as the moments of defeat you will face on your journey will feel just like that—defeat. Done. Not to be continued.

Give yourself grace when you are frustrated with your actions. Accept where you are and who you are *right now* to move forward. Shower yourself with compassion when you hit rock bottom. Choose to love yourself so deeply that giving up isn't a choice.

I want you to imagine yourself as a little kid learning how to be alive for the first time. Imagine you are going back and restarting and raising yourself from the ground up.

What would you do differently?

For starters, I bet you wouldn't yell at the child version of you for making a mistake. Instead, you'd give them grace. You'd know they are new to being human and you'd remind them it's safe to make mistakes. You'd tell them it's okay to proceed after a mistake.

You would get the opportunity to go back and let the little you cry when dealing with something heavy or difficult. You would remind them it's safe to feel and that crying isn't a sign of weakness.

You would shower them with love and affection when an experience made them feel insecure or less than and remind them of their worthiness no matter what anyone says or does.

We often think we are doing ourselves a favor when we harshly criticize ourselves, thinking it will motivate us to change or do better. We might even believe that if we speak kinder to ourselves, we will become "soft" or slack off. This could not be further from the truth. Self-criticism activates the brain's threat system and surges the cortisol levels in your body (your fight or flight hormone). Over time, this can lead to depression/anxiety, weight gain, intestinal problems, high blood pressure, and more. *You are not doing yourself a favor by being hard on yourself.*

You must learn to treat yourself with this type of gentleness. Harsh words and the emotion of shaming yourself repetitively will only hurt you. Imagine a child raised only with harsh words. A child who was shamed for everything. A child who was expected to be perfect. You can imagine how that child would end up.

The same thing happens to us when we continuously listen to our inner critic and when we allow it to take the reins and control us. We become a shell of who we are meant to be. Our light slowly goes out. We lose ourselves.

The self-criticism you inflict on yourself will never be worth it. Picking yourself apart will never make you feel better. You will **never** be better because of it. Self-criticism will keep you from stepping into the person you are meant to become.

Conclusion

I used to have this dread of getting older because I had this idea that I was going to *have* to conform to what everyone else was doing. I constantly heard the normalized language of complaint about adult life where people expressed extreme distaste for Monday and the thrill of it almost being Friday. Living a life you dread should not be a standard part of life. It's not why we are here on this Earth. We aren't here to be miserable and dread every day. And guess what? You CAN decide to do something different.

One of the most important, if not the most important realizations I had postgrad, was that I got to be the creator of my reality. I got to decide what my life was going to look like, what emotions I was going to feel, and every single thing else. I make the rules.

And yes, this sometimes comes with its hardships. As I explained in detail in the section of this book about courage, you need courage to live by your own rules. You might disappoint people in the process. You might upset people who want to control the outcome of your life. But the reward of listening to yourself is much greater than temporarily making people question you.

Fully and wholeheartedly believing in yourself is the cheat code to your success. There will be plenty of people out there challenging what it is you want to do. People will tell you to be realistic. To re-think what your dreams are. They will tell you that what you want to do is not a smart idea, it's not reasonable, and it's not going to work.

There will always be a surplus of people who think you are crazy, delusional, and destined to fail when you decide to do something out of the ordinary. And these people will not forget to remind you how they feel about what you are doing.

I want you to reframe the way you see people who do that to you. Initially, when someone doesn't believe in us, it hurts. We feel like no one has our back. We want to jump to conclusions that they are right, maybe we are delusional. Listen closely.

Michelle Lynn Johnson

The people who put you down about your dreams are the ones who do not believe in themselves. They limit themselves because they don't believe in their dreams, and in turn, they project that onto you. The limits they are speaking of have *nothing* to do with your dreams being unrealistic or delusional.

Sadly, the limits they have for themselves were likely projected onto them by their parents or teachers or anyone they looked up to as kids. Self-limiting projection is a generational cycle.

Being solely realistic will never bring you the life of your dreams. Being realistic will bring you complacency and comfort, which we now know is the recipe for staying the same. The recipe for feeling the same emotions, thinking the same thoughts, and doing the same things. Being realistic is not the route that brings the emotions you dream of feeling: passion, fulfillment, excitement, bliss, etc.

This is why you are going to choose to believe in yourself at a crazy level, to let yourself dream without limits, who chooses over and over again to believe in your capability and drown out the voices of everyone who says otherwise, *even if right now the voice saying otherwise is your own.*

This is the difference between what it will mean to live your dream life compared to your comfort zone life. You gain nothing from being realistic besides temporary comfort. You will gain everything from deciding to believe in yourself and your dreams. Your dreams are there for a reason. You didn't come up with them by accident. They were given to you for you to be here and accomplish.

The way I choose to look at things is imagining myself six months from now. I imagine what my life would be like in six months if I chose to delusionally believe in myself and my capability versus what my life would be like if I gave up on myself.

Doing this reminds me and puts into perspective the insane difference one decision can make. One decision to say, "Screw it, I'm going all in on myself," versus the decision to believe the people who told you your dreams were too crazy.

As we know from learning about the brain, we know our thoughts, emotions, and behaviors are all connected, and they create the reality we live in.

Imagine the difference in your reality if you decided to allow your thoughts to be about this new, seemingly crazy belief in yourself. You'd think things like, "Of course, things always work out for me," "Of course, I can love my life," or, "Of course, I am capable of doing everything I want to do." And in turn, you'd feel confident, excited, passionate, alive, motivated, and inspired. Well, you guessed it, when you feel those emotions, your behavior will include going out and finally acting towards your goals, finally doing the things you wanted to do, and actively creating your dream life.

Imagine if you had decided instead to not believe in yourself. Your thoughts would say, "Well, guess I'll never amount to anything," "They were right, I am not good enough," or, "I'll never be able to leave this town." You can guess the rest. Feelings of anxiety, depression, insecurity, and doom flood in. Then the behaviors—going through the motions, sleeping away your problems, lashing out at others, and becoming the person who brings themselves down. And maybe even *becoming the person who decides to remind other people they should be realistic.*

The difference in the two realities just by making two different but small decisions, is monumental.

This is why, starting today, no matter how hard it is to do at first, you are going to act as if you have this delusional self-confidence. You are going to start believing in yourself in a way that will probably feel extra crazy, and weird at first. It won't feel normal to you in the beginning, but it will eventually.

If you choose to speak out loud to those around you words that reflect your new self, understand you may be met with people who will criticize, talk about you behind your back, or try to "bring you back down to Earth." Be prepared to ignore them. Don't argue or try to be understood. Anyone who is threatened by your new self is not going to understand you no matter how much you try to explain yourself. Spare yourself the energy and just keep pushing forward, recognizing within your mind that it's nothing to take personally. Instead, remember to hear in their voice that it is their inner critic projecting outward onto you.

The best route to take when you are on the journey to becoming the best version of yourself and creating your dream life is to just let your actions and the results of your actions do the talking. People will see how well this self-belief and newfound confidence has done for you. Finding the strength to validate and believe in yourself no matter what any outside source says to you, is what is going to change your circumstances. Self-belief has unbelievable power that will unlock your wildest dreams.

All things considered, although postgrad may be a journey filled with peaks and valleys, my wish is that you take with you the lessons that make the dips to the valleys a bit easier, and you feel inspired to create a life you are insanely excited about. Life is meant to be enjoyed and you are meant to experience all of the beautiful things it has to offer you. If you take just one action from this book, promise me that you will agree to always push forward in the moments you want to give up on yourself. All it takes is one little step and one agreement with yourself to keep going for you to see massive change. No matter what your mind tries to convince you of, remember that you are capable and worthy of everything you desire.

You might have periods during your journey where you feel a little lost again. Where you forget all of this, where you become stuck being controlled by your limiting beliefs, where you lack inspiration, and where you become disconnected from the version of you that wanted to live your dreams. Sometimes that is just the way life is. Please remember the importance of showing yourself the compassion and grace I mentioned. It's okay to get off track. Just remember why you started any of this in the first place and understand it will never be too late to begin again. Pick up this book whenever you need it and allow it to remind you of your capability to live out your dreams at any point. You are more powerful than you can even comprehend at this moment—choose to believe it even if you don't yet feel it.

Extra resources to guide you on your journey

Positive affirmations are a powerful tool that guides us along our journey of growth. If you've never heard of positive affirmations, they are short statements that help challenge your brain to reframe irrational/negative thoughts and create a healthier mindset. Although these affirmations may feel silly at first when we don't quite believe them, when practiced consistently over time we are more likely to see them as our new truth.

If we are working on self-love or confidence, choosing affirmations that align with those issues will guide us in creating a mindset that reflects the qualities we are looking to further develop within ourselves. Choose affirmations that most resonate with you and implement them daily, whether you journal them, speak them to yourself in the mirror, speak them in your head while you go for a walk, speak them into a voice memo while you're driving in traffic, etc. Affirmations are an excellent way to fill your thoughts with substance instead of letting your mind drift into negativity during the day. It's important to be intentional with what you allow your mind to think while you work to create a healthy mindset and implement new habits. This prevents your mind from wandering, thinking about meaningless things, and possibly upsetting yourself just out of habit (remember what we learned about how our brains choose thoughts out of habit!).

Not only this, but it will be important to get into the habit of choosing thoughts that comfort you and ease your emotions when going on this difficult but rewarding journey of self-development. Here is your very own list of affirmation ideas to use in your journey. If they don't resonate, choose different ones or create your own, it's in your hands! The idea is around what you are saying to feel good and feel aligned.

Affirmations for difficult days:[9]

1. I am doing the best I can do at this time.
2. It is healthy and necessary for me to take the time to heal, no matter what that may look like for me.
3. It is safe for me to let go of what no longer serves me.
4. I love and accept myself wholeheartedly, just as I am right now.
5. I am healing by allowing myself grace.

159

6. I release self-judgment because I am allowed to take the time to rest. My body needs extra rest when times are tough.

7. My worth is not based on my productivity; I understand that I am worthy of love and compassion even when I am not doing anything at all.

8. Small steps are better than no steps, and I am making progress every day just by pushing through.

9. I believe in myself and my ability to push through difficult times.

10. I can overcome any challenge life throws my way, and I will continue to be gentle with myself during the times when struggles appear.

Affirmations for confidence:

1. I walk into every room with confidence, and I allow myself to take up space.

2. I radiate confidence, and my presence is valuable.

3. I speak with ease, and I always know what to say to others.

4. I am secure in who I am and what I stand for.

5. My power and capabilities are unlimited; I will always choose to believe in myself.

6. All I need to succeed is within me, I am my source of power.

7. My energy is magnetic and captivating.

8. I am free from self-doubt and filled with self-confidence.

9. My validation is enough for me; I recognize external validation cannot determine my self-worth.

10. I feel more and more confident every day.

Affirmations for self-love:

1. My inner beauty shines through my words and presence.

2. Loving myself comes easily and naturally.

3. I am open to receiving love from myself and others.

4. I am strong in the boundaries I set, and I expect others to respect them.

5. My feelings deserve to be expressed and I allow them to be felt.

6. I allow myself to love exactly who I am, including all of my shortcomings. Each part of myself deserves love and acceptance.

7. My body tells me what it needs, and I am willing to listen.

8. I allow myself to accept love, abundance, and prosperity.

9. I am proud of myself for pushing through every day and I love myself for doing so.

10. I allow myself to freely be my most authentic self, no matter what anyone thinks.

Affirmations for self-compassion:

1. I understand that difficult times arise to allow me to shed old layers so I can level up into a better version of myself.
2. I am grateful I am shown old wounds I need to heal when they rise up in difficult times, this happens for my higher good.
3. I realize there will always be ups and downs in life, but I know the difficult times are there to teach me and the highs will always return.
4. I am patient with myself when I am struggling; I recognize my body needs more rest during times of healing.
5. My mistakes are there to teach me, I see them as a positive instead of a negative.
6. I recognize that not every day I will be able to perform at my best, but I recognize my ability to always try.
7. I am enough as I am, even when I feel my worst.
8. I am allowed to feel hurt and upset, but I recognize I have the strength within me to overcome those feelings.
9. Negative emotions and thoughts will pass through me without judging myself for feeling them.
10. I am always improving because I am always learning from my struggles.

Affirmations for abundance:

1. I am grateful for all of the abundance I have received in my life and for all of the abundance I will continue to receive.
2. I am the kind of person who always attracts the most amazing people and opportunities.
3. I am receiving abundance in so many different ways, and I am so lucky.
4. Abundance flows to me quickly, easily, and all the time.
5. I am able and open to seeing all opportunities to create more abundance in my life.
6. I am putting value into the world, and I am rewarded for it.
7. I am aligned with the energy of abundance.
8. I am open to all of the ways abundance can flow to me.
9. I let go of any negativity I have been carrying with me about my ability to create wealth and abundance.
10. There is more than enough abundance in the world for me, the possibilities are endless.

Affirmations for negative thoughts:

1. I have a deep inner strength that allows me to feel and know that I am not controlled by my thoughts, my thoughts are controlled by me.
2. I release all resistance I may have towards changing and growing into a new version of myself, I understand that it will be worth it to push through the times it feels uncomfortable to grow.
3. I have control over what I focus on, I am intentional about the things I choose to give power to.
4. I understand the negative thoughts I am experiencing are due to old patterns coming up, I can let these thoughts pass without judgment.
5. I understand that my thoughts are not who I am, and that uncomfortable thoughts are not a reflection of my character.
6. I can choose to shift into more positive perspectives when I find myself spiraling.
7. Negative thoughts flow away quickly because I have the strength to pay them no mind.
8. Instead of fearing my negative thoughts, I remind myself I am the one with the power to choose how I want to think going forward.
9. I consistently choose to ask myself, "What is the best thing that could happen?"
10. I fully and wholeheartedly know everything is always working out in my favor whether I can see it now or not.

Journaling ideas:

Journaling is an excellent way to improve your mindset and learn yourself on a deeper level. Journal prompts are a great way to get started when you aren't sure what to write about. Included below are various journal prompts to get you started.

Journal prompts for self-exploration:

1. What are your biggest self-sabotaging activities? Can you change these? What can you replace them with?
2. What do you want to be remembered for and how can you become that person?
3. What boundaries do you need to set with yourself and others to achieve your goals?
4. When do you feel the most confident and the least confident? How can you create more instances of confidence?
5. How can you love yourself better?

6. What is something you struggle to follow through with and why do you struggle to do it?

7. What are a few things that cause anxiety for you? Identify the triggers if possible and brainstorm ideas for overcoming these situations if they happen.

8. Describe the last time you went out of your comfort zone. Brainstorm an idea to do it again.

9. Describe an activity you have always wanted to do. Why haven't you done it yet? How can you plan to do it?

10. What are you most proud of in your life?

11. What are your passions? If you feel you have none, begin to write about when you started to feel disconnected from yourself. Was it childhood? When did you stop feeling inspired? How can you get reinspired?

12. What does success mean to you?

13. How are you *really* doing? Be honest with yourself. Is there someone you would feel comfortable sharing this with? If not, why?

14. Who do you admire most and why?

15. Who do you appreciate most in your life?

16. What type of connections do you want to make with others? What feels meaningful to you in relationships with friends, family, or a significant other?

17. Who are you at your core? Not who you identify as (student, job title). Truly, at your core, who are you? Do you know? If not, think of ways you can better get to know yourself. Core qualities could be compassionate, thoughtful, honest, loyal, selfless, forgiving, enthusiastic, empathetic, courageous, loving, self-aware, patient, ambitious, etc.

18. What new skills do you want to learn?

19. When have you felt passion and excitement in your life? Describe the situation and why it caused you to feel those emotions. When was the last time you felt that way? Can you create more instances going forward to feel more of those emotions?

20. What activities cause you to forget time and reality? If you don't have any, brainstorm ideas for what you think could be something you could do that would get your full attention and truly excite you.

Deep inner-healing exercises:

Shadow work

What is **shadow work**? Psychoanalyst Carl Jung first developed the concept of shadow work as a way to help people create wholeness within themselves. He believed that everyone has a "shadow self," meaning a version of ourselves we repress and don't want to acknowledge.[8] Shadow work is asking yourself questions to uncover parts of yourself you may be ashamed of, hide from, or see as a negative part of yourself. Everyone has a shadow. Doing shadow work can allow us to reveal that part of ourselves and heal from what may have caused it to arise in the first place. Digging deep and facing our shadow self is an incredible way to feel true self-acceptance and cultivate a deep bond with ourselves. If we reject the parts of us we are ashamed of, we will never feel fully whole. Facing our shadow takes bravery and vulnerability, but it will allow for immense inner growth and healing.

Disclaimer: Shadow work is intense, emotional work. It requires a certain level of self-honesty that may be triggering for some people. It often brings up a lot of emotions. Be sure to do this when you are in a good state of mind or even with a professional if you are sensitive to re-living the past or diving deep emotionally. Go at your own pace and do only what you feel ready for.

Journal prompts for shadow work:

1. What do you think are the worst traits a person can embody? Have you shown these traits before? If so, when? Why does it bother you so much when other people have these traits?
2. What emotion do you most avoid? What emotion is the worst for you to feel and what times do you find this emotion coming up most? What do you do to avoid it?
3. Do you notice yourself avoiding it when it happens?
4. Name a time you acted in a way that was toxic or unhealthy in a relationship with someone you care about—friend, family, or romantic partner. Is this behavior a pattern for you? Are you aware of it when you are doing it? How can you work on this?
5. Who do you envy most and why? When does this come up for you? How do you act when you feel envious?
6. Do you consider yourself to be confrontational? Do you like this about yourself whether you are or aren't? Why do you think you are that way?
7. What misconception do people have about you that bothers you the most?
8. Do you generally feel like you are on an even playing field with other people or do you feel less than or better than other people? Who do you feel are your equals and why? If you think you are better, who are the people you feel are less than you and why? If you think you are less than, who are the people that are better and why?
9. Name a time you felt most ashamed of yourself. What did you do? What triggered you to do it? Consciously allow yourself self-forgiveness. How can you avoid doing this again? Would you do it again?

10. Are there qualities of your parents/caregivers that you resent? Do you think you embody any of these qualities?

11. What does failure mean to you?

12. Is there anyone in your life who has belittled or invalidated your emotions? How did that make you feel?

13. What emotions bring out the worst in you? What triggers these emotions and what behaviors does it cause?

14. With whom or in what situation do you feel like you can't be your true self, or do you notice you pretend to be someone you're not? Why do you do it? Can you see yourself acting differently in the future?

15. How do you handle disappointment?

16. How do you feel when others express their anger? How do you express anger?

17. When have you felt most betrayed in your life? Have you dealt with that?

18. What kind of self-destructive behaviors do you take part in?

19. What are your pet peeves in other people and what do you judge people for most? Do you see any of those things in yourself?

20. Write about a difficult childhood memory that you remember vividly. Why do you think it stuck with you so much?

21. What is your most painful memory?

Self-growth 30-day challenges: Use the journal at the back of the book to document your experience.

Commit to doing one thing out of your comfort zone that aids in helping you become the person you want to be every single day. The more you get comfortable with getting uncomfortable, the quicker you will see drastic growth within yourself.

Complete a visualization meditation each day where you spend at least 5 minutes visualizing yourself as who you want to become and what you want your life to look like. It can be helpful to find a video online to guide you through the process. Search "Visualization Meditation." Research has shown that visualizing is a powerful way to engage your brain to overcome limiting beliefs and implement healthy habits.

Go out of your way to do something kind for someone else every single day. Put someone's cart away at the store, share a compliment you might have otherwise been too afraid to say, or drop off a coffee to a friend. This challenge will help you feel fulfilled from things outside of yourself—a key component in creating happiness.

Journal every single day. Whether it's for five minutes or an hour, take the time to choose a journal prompt and write. If none of the journal prompts stand out to you, just do a brain dump on everything that is going on within your mind. The goal is to further expand your self-knowledge so you can build a deeper connection with yourself.

Get inspired daily. Find speeches, podcasts, or videos that spark passion within you and remind you why you want to change in the first place. By doing this, you will cultivate that feeling of inspiration and excitement each day and drastically improve the way you feel and the progress you will make.

Self-forgiveness exercise: Holding shame and guilt from the past within your mind and body can hinder you greatly when creating a new beginning for yourself. This exercise can be used with any situation you may need to forgive yourself for. Examples include something you did to someone or yourself that causes you to feel bad about yourself, shame/guilt you are holding from a situation, regrets for not taking a specific action, etc.

1. **Choose what it is you want to forgive yourself for.** Be as detailed as you wish in the explanation. Getting specific with details and re-living a painful situation can be difficult, but being honest with yourself will allow you to begin to release those heavy feelings.

_____

_____

_____

_____

_____

_____

_____

_____

_____

2. **Reflect on the situation.** Was there a reason you did what you did? Did you instantly regret it, or did it take time for you to realize you were in the wrong? Why is this situation still playing on your mind so heavily? Now is not the time to make excuses for yourself. Remember, no one is here in this workbook judging you. It's your safe space to be open and honest.

_____

_____

_____

_____

_____

_____

_____

_____

_____

3. **How has this affected you since it happened?** Has it created any negative beliefs about yourself? Caused you to feel or think a certain way? Has it changed your behavior at all?

_____

_____

_____

_____

_____

_____

_____

_____

4. Is there anything you can do today to help tie up loose ends in the situation and move forward?

_____

_____

_____

_____

_____

_____

_____

5. Look at the situation from a new perspective. If you still feel shame or guilt about a past situation you are likely carrying a negative or even irrational belief about it. Let's look at the facts to help you see it in a new light:

-Humans are allowed to make mistakes, there is not a human on this Earth who has never made a mistake.

-You are older and wiser now than you were in the past or even yesterday. Do not beat yourself up for doing what you knew best at the time.

-Doing something wrong or making a bad decision in the past does not mean you are a bad person. Especially if you are the type of person to carry guilt and feel bad about something for this long, you are _not_ a bad person. Bad people do not feel remorse.

-You are allowed to let go of the past and use it to teach you how to be better today and in your future. No one is chaining you to the events of the past and forcing you to be defined by them forever. Your mind is the only thing doing that.

Repeat this to yourself:

"I am ready to forgive myself for my mistakes and I allow myself to grow and learn from my past."

"I give myself permission to heal and let go of the shame I have been holding from making this mistake."

6. **Allow yourself grace.** Write yourself a kind and compassionate letter as if you were sending a letter of forgiveness to a close friend who you still deeply love and cherish.

_____

_____

_____

_____

_____

_____

_____

_____

_____

_____

_____

_____

_____

_____

_____

_____

_____

_____

_____

_____

_____

_____

Get out of your overthinking spiral: Sometimes when you start overthinking it feels like nothing can stop it. You might try to shift your thoughts to healthier ones over and over again, but yet your mind can't seem to stop wandering back to the original fears and worries. Being someone who used to chronically overthink everything, I created an exercise to help get your spiraling thoughts out of your head and onto paper. If the thoughts are going to occur, we might as well transfer them onto paper so we can take a better look at what is *really* going on under the surface.

Explain the situation you are overthinking about. Imagine you are going to sit down with a friend and explain what is going on with you to get advice on what to do. Write down in detail everything that has been going through your head. Write down every "what if" thought, every self-deprecating thought, every irrational thought that makes no sense. Whatever is going on in your head, put it into words on paper.

_____

_____

_____

_____

_____

_____

_____

_____

_____

_____

_____

_____

_____

_____

_____

_____

_____

_____

Can you pinpoint when these thoughts began? Are they stemming from the past (anxiety about an event that already occurred) or are they fears about the future (anxiety about an event that has yet to occur)? What feels most distressing about this situation?

_____

_____

_____

_____

_____

_____

_____

_____

Overthinking is our way of feeling in control. We feel we may discover new information or stumble upon an epiphany that will suddenly ease our minds. However, I want to share with you an understanding that may help you choose a different route of action. When we overthink, the thoughts that are running through our minds are jumbled, chaotic, and often irrational. When our thoughts are like this, we aren't going to find any new rational answers for ourselves. If we want to feel a sense of control that can lead to a positive outcome, we can take ourselves outside of the situation. Let's start here:

Write down any evidence you have for how the situation could *actually* play out based on what you know about the past. How often does what you are overthinking about happen? How often has it happened to you in the past? For example, if you have the fear you were acting embarrassing last weekend and therefore are jumping to the conclusion you're a horrible person and everyone hates you, try and see if you can pinpoint concrete evidence that this is what happened or is going to happen:

Okay, so now you can see for yourself *outside* of what is going on in your mind that there isn't much that is rational about what you are thinking. But, if you are still convinced that these thoughts *are* your truth, we can take it a step further:

Look at the situation as if your friend were describing it about them. Would you think they were going to have the same outcome? Or would you recognize that a mistake in the past or fear about the future doesn't and won't define their whole life?

How would you help them get through it if it did occur? Is this something you believe they could get through? This can help you understand that our minds often choose to catastrophize situations more than makes rational sense.

_____

_____

_____

_____

_____

_____

_____

Cognitive distortion is when our mind pushes an irrational or negative narrative with no real evidence or fact that it is true. This is often occurring when we enter those dreaded overthinking spirals. Breaking it down like this can help us see what is fact and what is irrational.

The remaining space in the book is your journal. Answer journal prompts, write creatively, and reflect on your experiences—whatever you wish. I hope you see this as a safe space for you to deepen and explore your bond with yourself while you go on this journey of inner growth.

Journal

_____

_____

_____

_____

_____

_____

_____

_____

_____

_____

_____

_____

_____

_____

_____

_____

_____

_____

_____

_____

_____

_____

_____

_____

_____

_____

_____

_____

_____

_____

_____

_____

_____

_____

Michelle Lynn Johnson

Michelle Lynn Johnson

Michelle Lynn Johnson

Michelle Lynn Johnson

Michelle Lynn Johnson

Michelle Lynn Johnson

Shift Your Standards

Michelle Lynn Johnson

Michelle Lynn Johnson

Michelle Lynn Johnson

Michelle Lynn Johnson

_____

_____

_____

_____

_____

_____

_____

_____

_____

_____

_____

_____

_____

_____

_____

_____

_____

_____

References

[1] Vilhauer, J. PhD. (2020, September 27). How Your Thinking Creates Your Reality. *Psychology Today.*

[2] Eagleman, D. (2016). *The Brain: The Story of You.* Canongate Books.

[3] Gulati, A. (2015). Understanding neurogenesis in the adult human brain. *Indian Journal of Pharmacology,* 47(6), 583. https://doi.org/10.4103/0253-7613.169598

[4] McLachlan, S. (2021, December 22). The science of habit: how to rewire your brain. *Healthline.* https://www.healthline.com/health/the-science-of-habit#1

[5] Houghton, A. (2002). How do we limit ourselves? The BMJ, 324(7341), S107. https://www.ncbi.nlm.nih.gov/pmc/articles/PMC10392899/

[6] Eagleman, D. (2016). *Incognito: The Secret Lives of the Brain.* Canongate Canons.

[7] Dispenza, J. (2015). *Breaking the Habit of Being Yourself: How to Lose Your Mind and Create a New One.* Hay House.

[8] Lonngi, G. (2024). The Jungian Shadow and Self-Acceptance. Tamug.edu. https://www.tamug.edu/nautilus/articles/The%20Jungian%20Shadow%20and%20Self-Acceptance.html

[9] The Science Behind Self-Affirmations | *Psychology Today.* (n.d.). Www.psychologytoday.com. https://www.psychologytoday.com/us/blog/the-age-of-overindulgence/202307/the-science-behind-self-affirmations

Follow the author:

Author Michelle Lynn Johnson is certified in Rational Emotive Behavioral Therapy and Mindset Life Coaching via Transformation Academy 2021. Check out www.michelleljohnson.com to get the latest information and resources, and to join the postgrad community on social media. You will find all of Michelle's social media links on her website.